MW00457384

Eerie Quad Cities

Eerie
QUAD CITIES

Michael McCarty and John Brassard Jr.

Illustrations by Jason McLean; Introduction by The Amazing Kreskin

THE
History
PRESS

Published by The History Press
Charleston, SC
www.historypress.com

First published 2021

Manufactured in the United States

ISBN 9781467147477

Library of Congress Control Number: 2021938595

*To The Amazing Kreskin, who has always been amazing
and will continue to amaze all.*

Contents

CONTENTS

Foreword

The writing and release of Michael McCarty's sequel to his first book, *Ghosts of the Quad Cities*, is ironic. The timing could never have been planned or anticipated since he was writing this book as a sequel long before the pandemic crisis swept the world.

The loss of life here in the Western world has been disastrous, just as it was in many other countries. If this current book, *Eerie Quad Cities*, had not been planned as a sequel to Mike's first writing, it would be easy to credit Mike with the remarkable timing of psychic intuition.

By the end of March 2020, I could foresee some of the key sociological changes and developments that the disastrous experiences affecting the nations of the world would bring about. The result—the reawakening of interest by thousands of people to attend séances—is taking place now and will continue even after you read this today. You do not have to believe or disbelieve in séances. You do not have to question whether talking to the dead and such activities are real or not. Whatever your feelings about these things, people of various ages and all over the world continue to show an interest in them. This can be seen in various mediums, ranging from movies and literature to simple conversations around the dinner table. One has only to study cultural history to learn that after great wars and losses of population—whether you go back to 1918 or after the world wars—there has been interest both in real life and in fiction in the subject matter and activity of spirit communication and talking to the dead.

The Amazing Kreskin has mystified and entertained millions all over the world with his live two-hour one-man shows. Kreskin has also starred in his own TV show, *The Amazing World of Kreskin*, and has a record-setting hundreds of television appearances on shows hosted by Joey Bishop, Mike Douglas, Steve Allen, Johnny Carson (he even inspired Carson's skit "The Great Carnac"), Dinah Shore, Phil Donahue, Larry King, Howard Stern and Jimmy Fallon. *Courtesy of The Amazing Kreskin.*

The pandemic left us without funerals, and most cultures have customs that prepare us to carry through our experience of the burial of the deceased that we know and love. There are scores of people in my Polish and Italian family, and the wakes were extremely meaningful and memorable for us, as they gave the living an opportunity to say goodbye. Even as a kid, I learned at the wakes—hearing stories, conversations and discussions, including wild, crazy incidents that were told to honor the life of the person who had passed. Look at the Jewish people, whose mourners sit shiva for seven days to be a support to those who were closest to the deceased person. Look at the lengths that we have gone to at times to recover the bodies of fallen soldiers. Some involved searches in countries where our military lost its troops. We have seen in past months people who were dying in hospitals alone, except for the medical staff attending. They could not express a farewell to those whom they loved.

Funerals, if they were to take place, had to be postponed—sometimes for weeks, sometimes for months. What happens when we have lost our methods of saying goodbye? The séance, for whatever it's worth, has been and will increasingly be accessed by thousands of people. This is simply human nature—a seeking, an interest in a way of communicating.

It is the very nature of humans to not only achieve closer feelings toward those we have loved but also have some kind of defined separation from those we have lost. They are part of our history, and we are not used to suddenly erasing part of the world that they helped build. To not have some sense of completion would leave most people with a feeling of deep guilt. Michael McCarty and John Brassard Jr.'s *Eerie Quad Cities* could not have appeared at a more appropriate, harmonious and key moment in current modern history.

Above: The Amazing Kreskin once did a séance at the Phi Kappa Chi fraternity house in 1991. In the summer of 2020, the frat house was leveled. *Photo by Michael McCarty.*

Right: The Amazing Kreskin in his office, reading *Ghosts of the Quad Cities* by Michael McCarty and Mark McLaughlin. Kreskin also wrote the introduction to that book. *Courtesy of The Amazing Kreskin.*

FOREWORD

I love mystery. I am fascinated with the unknown and, at times, overwhelmed by the unexplained. That is not a warning—it is a promise. You are about to take a voyage into a remarkably mysterious world.

In Mike's first book, *Ghosts of the Quad Cities*, he recounted the story of our gathering at the frat house Phi Kappa Chi at Palmer College in Davenport, Iowa. That scenario has a further irony given what is taking place at the present time. The séance was dramatic, and all who joined had memorable experiences, but I am addressing at this moment the present situation. Palmer College leveled the houses on the block, including the Phi Kappa Chi house. Was the cause of the strange happenings experienced by those who lived there destroyed with the house, or are they tied to the property itself? What if the underpinnings carry magnetic memories and vibes for whatever had brought on the previous phenomena experienced there? It will be interesting if sensitive people report strange moods overtaking them as they pass over or occupy the space above that area.

Now, don't misunderstand me. I am not attacking those who leveled the Phi Kappa Chi chapter house, although I think it's a loss and I hope that the real estate people do not replace the setting with an ice skating rink. Let me say here that I am ready to predict that some unexplained phenomena will take place in the years to come over the area where the Phi Kappa Chi chapter house was set. That I foresee.

—THE AMAZING KRESKIN,
Summer of 2020

Preface

Welcome to the eerie side of the Quad Cities.

Imagine this: Michael McCarty and John Brassard Jr. are going to lead you through a dark maze. It doesn't matter where you go: a haunted house, an abandoned nursing home, a spooky cemetery. There are ghosts, banshees, giants, Bigfoot, UFOs and strange animals and creatures here. Some can be explained, and others have no rational explanation. Along the way, we will whisper soft words in your ear, encouraging you to journey into the dark places that chill your bones.

Teaming Mike and John up together to write this book was an act of pure magic. John, a local historian (the Kitchen Table Historian, with a website, blogs and a podcast) is the author of such books as *Murder and Mayhem in Scott County* and coauthor of *Scott County Cemeteries* (with John Brassard Sr.), and he was on *The Dead Files* in October 2020. Mike is the author of more than forty-five books, including nonfiction books about the paranormal such as *Ghosts of the Quad Cities* (with Mark McLaughlin) and *Ghostly Tales of Route 66* (with Connie Corcoran Wilson); his book *Conversations with Kreskin* (with The Amazing Kreskin) was featured on *Late Night with Jimmy Fallon*.

This is also a very personal book for Michael McCarty and John Brassard Jr., both of whom wanted to share their own ghostly encounters.

FROM MICHAEL MCCARTY:

Although I did write about some of my ghostly encounters or unexplained occurrences while researching *Ghosts of the Quad Cities*, there was one personal story that I didn't put in that book that I want to share here.

Michael McCarty (*left*) and John Brassard Jr. (*right*) at the *Ghosts of the Quad Cities* book signing at the Book Rack, Davenport, Iowa. *Photo by Cindy McCarty.*

Back when I worked for the Funny Bone Comedy Club as a promotion coordinator, I also performed in an acoustic group that consisted of myself, my cousin Ron and a good friend of mine named Renee. We called ourselves the Carnival of Souls, after a low-budget 1960s black-and-white horror movie. Renee played the keyboard, but since the band was just acoustic, she only sang.

Eventually, she wanted to learn to play the guitar, so I offered to teach her. The only problem was that she was left-handed, and I had only right-handed guitars. So, I taught her to play with the opposite hand, unlike a lot of lefties who played right-handed guitars (like Jimi Hendrix, Duane Allman, Elvis Costello, Joe Perry, Johnny Winters, Mark Knopfler and Billy Corgan). I had an old right-handed guitar I loaned her so she could further her practicing and playing and songwriting.

When my wife and I were living at our old apartment, Renee would come to visit us from Iowa City. Since it was about an hour-long trip, the first thing she did was hit the bathroom.

A few years later, Renee passed away at the age of twenty-seven. I was devastated—so were a lot of people. She was such a fun, loving and great person to be around. And she was one hell of a talented singer and songwriter. I heard from a mutual friend of ours that her mother wanted me to pick up my old guitar that I loaned her. I really didn't mind because it was just a beater and I had other guitars.

Shortly after Renee had passed on, one of the strange things that my wife and I noticed was that the water in the bathroom sink would often be running. Both the hot and cold faucets were always turned on right in the middle. It had happened about half a dozen or so times.

Then things got stranger. One evening, at the dinner table, my wife said, "What the—." Her left earring had fallen onto the table. And my wife said that she felt like someone was behind her and pushed it out. To make things even stranger, these were earrings that Renee had given to my wife as a gift about two weeks before she died.

The last unusual thing that happened took place on Christmas. My wife had already left to see her family. I had a splitting headache, so I took an Ibuprofen and waited for it to kick in. I was all alone in the apartment, and it was quiet—the apartment building was empty because everyone was visiting family on the holiday.

Then, suddenly, I heard a noise coming from the bathroom. It was quiet at first and then started to get a little louder. I went into the bathroom and found the water in the bathroom sink running. Both the hot and cold faucets were always turned on right in the middle.

About a week after Christmas, I went to Clinton to pick up my guitar. Then nothing strange happened again. No water faucets mysteriously turning on. No earrings being poked out of my wife's ears. It is my opinion that Renee was trying to contact me and let me know that she wanted me to have my old guitar back that I loaned her. Once I got the guitar back, she no longer needed to communicate with me.

FROM JOHN BRASSARD JR.:

I have experienced things that I cannot fully explain. In 2002, I took a trip to Mount Carmel Cemetery, an enormous old Catholic cemetery just outside Chicago. It's extremely well maintained and serves as the final home of both the good and the infamous. A friend of mine and I had decided to go to see the final resting place of several Prohibition-era gangsters buried there.

The first one we saw was Al Capone, probably the best known of them all. After that, we found Dion O'Bannon, the leader of the North Side Gang. For me, that's when things started to get weird.

As you can imagine, I've been to more cemeteries than I can think about over the years, from private family plots in rural Iowa to truly massive graveyards with tens of thousands of interments. I've been in them at night and at all hours in between. Cemeteries do not freak me out.

And yet, as I approached the large stone obelisk that marks O'Bannon's grave, a strange feeling came over me. It took me a little while to place it, but when I did, I was genuinely surprised. I felt...*unwelcome*. I felt tolerated. I felt like something didn't really want me there but didn't have much choice in the matter. Even without choice, whatever it was didn't have to be happy about it. At the same time, I also had this very clear idea that whatever it was also demanded that I be respectful. It may not have been able to force me to leave, but I was going to mind myself while I was there.

Honestly, I thought it was all in my head. For whatever reason, I couldn't shake that impression no matter what I did. I didn't want to tell my friend because I felt silly as hell for feeling that way. I was a historian for crying out loud!

We keep the stories of the dead. We share them with the living and remember the lost and forgotten. Cemeteries are part and parcel of that. Why on earth would I feel unwelcome there among the tombstones when I never had that feeling before anywhere else I had ever been?

I'm always respectful at cemeteries anyway, but that day I was almost formal in my actions. In almost all of the pictures we took that day, I stood rigid and unsmiling.

One of the last graves we visited that day was of Sam Giancana, who headed the Chicago Outfit for several years. He had a reputation for being a violent and bloody man and was definitely not someone to be trifled with. When I started to approach his burial place, I stopped cold. What was an uncomfortable feeling before was now a sensation of outright hostility. For the first and only time ever in a graveyard, it took a conscious effort of my will to approach the tomb and then to turn my back on it for a picture. Even now, almost twenty years later, I still clearly remember that feeling.

A week or so later, I was back at my home at Iowa State. The feelings, while still disconcerting when I thought about them, were easily dispelled in the full daylight of my home six hours away from where I had them.

A friend of mine was visiting, and I was telling her about the trip. I hadn't been through the photos yet, so we decided to look through them together.

Everything was fine until I reached the second picture that I had taken of the Genna brothers' mausoleum. The Genna brothers were Chicago bootleggers during Prohibition and used to pay people to make booze for them out of their own homes. Although it was a lucrative endeavor for them, a few of the brothers came to violent, bloody ends during that period.

It was a bright, sunny day in February when the picture was taken. There was no mist or rain that day at any point. Everything was perfectly clear. Still, there was an anomaly in the photo. There are two benches outside their mausoleum, one on either side. My friend decided to sit on one while the picture was taken, and the other was obviously empty. Well, at least it was in the first picture.

In the second, there is a mist on the second bench, roughly the size of, but not the shape of, a person. I started, shocked into silence. I knew what I was looking at, but I wouldn't allow my brain to form the thought into words. My friend, fascinated, did it for me.

"Oh! Looks like you got a ghost picture," she said, matter-of-factly.

The spell broken, I replied weakly, "Yes. Yes, it is."

I have no explanation for either my feelings that day or the picture. Could it have simply been my imagination and some kind of mental fatigue? Possibly. Or was it what I mentioned earlier, something *other*, something that I still can't explain to this day? Maybe the spirits of such violent men who, in life, demanded respect from those around them were still doing so from beyond the grave.

I've never been back to Mount Carmel. I've driven past it on the way into Chicago a time or two, but I've never quite gotten up enough nerve to go back and visit.

Sometimes, we believe what we want to believe in order to explain our own feelings. We get scared, and we convince ourselves that something really was watching us. Others, understanding the power of those feelings, manipulate them to their own ends. A place was never haunted, but that doesn't mean that we can't make up a really cool story that says it was.

Other times, however, we touch on something else. We brush up against something beyond our understanding, something that we can't begin to explain. It requires no back story, no reason for being.

I'm not here to preach you a sermon or to wow you with scientific splendor. I'm a simple historian and storyteller. Maybe you'll believe what I experienced that day and maybe you won't. Maybe you have a valid explanation where I have none.

Whatever you believe and however you feel, the stories are there.

So what is the Quad Cities? There are actually five cities, not four: Davenport and Bettendorf, Iowa, and Rock Island, Moline and East Moline, Illinois. Originally called the "Tri-Cities" with Davenport, Iowa, and Rock Island and Moline, Illinois, it became the Quad Cities with the addition of East Moline. As Bettendorf, Iowa, grew, it became part of the Quad Cities too. The name "Quint Cities" never caught on, as it still remains "the Quads."

In the surrounding areas in Illinois, you'll find Silvis, Milan, Hampton, Carbon Cliff, Port Byron, Andalusia, Coal Valley and Colona. On the other side of the Mississippi River in Iowa, there is Eldridge, Long Grove, Park View, Blue Grass, Buffalo, Walcott, Maysville, Mount Joy, Pleasant Valley, Le Claire, Panorama Park and Riverdale.

For nearly two centuries, towns and villages have been in the area, not counting the Native Americans, who lived in these areas many more centuries before that.

The area is famous for John Deere tractors; the Rock Island Arsenal, which is the largest government-owned weapons manufacturer in the entire country; and Lock and Dam No. 15, the longest roller dam in existence, which stretches between Arsenal Island in Rock Island and Davenport, Iowa. Every summer, the PGA Tour is played at the John Deere Classic in Moline, Illinois.

Michael McCarty and Mark McLaughlin wrote a lot about the Quad Cities in *Ghosts of the Quad Cities*, and John Brassard and John Brassard Jr. wrote about the area in *Scott County Cemeteries*. Here are some fun facts about the bi-state area:

- Happy Joe's pizza invented the taco pizza.
- Whitey's Ice Cream invented cookie dough ice cream.
- President Ronald Reagan began his radio career at WOC in Davenport. He lived at the Kimball House Hotel at 204 East Fourth Street from October to December 1932.
- Walt Disney applied for his first job in Davenport and was turned down. He saw an ad for a cartoonist in a trade journal and was interviewed by Alex F. Victor (of Victor Animatograph), a pioneer in 16mm film, but he didn't get the position.
- The show *American Pickers* originated in the Quad Cities.

There have been many celebrities who have hailed from the Quad Cities: jazz musician Bix Beiderbecke; actors Ken Berry and Eddie Albert and actresses Lara Flynn Boyle and Mary Beth Peil; comedian Tammy

Statue of Black Hawk by Welsh sculptor David Richards at the Black Hawk State Historic Site, commonly referred to as the Black Hawk State Park, in Rock Island, Illinois. *Photo by Michael McCarty.*

Pescatelli, who began her comedy career at the Funny Bone Comedy Club in Davenport (where Michael McCarty was working at the time); Denise Nickerson, a former Davenport resident who portrayed Violet Beauregarde in the 1971 film *Willy Wonka*; author JoAnna Lund; Native American warrior Black Hawk; William "Buffalo Bill" Cody; Pulitzer Prize–winning playwright and theater pioneer Susan Glaspell; gangster John Looney; tractor manufacturer John Deere; WWE wrestling superstar Seth Rollins; disc jockey William "Spike" O'Dell (better known as "Spike at the Mike"); artists John and Isabel Bloom; David Daniel Palmer (of Palmer College of Chiropractic); jazz drummer Louis Bellson; Roger Craig, football player with the San Francisco 49ers (when he was with the team, they won three Super Bowl titles, and Craig made NFL history by topping one thousand years in both running and receiving); boxer Michael Nunn; William Velie, who founded the Velie Carriage Company and Velie Motor Vehicle Company and invented the airplane Velie Moncoup, which won the U.S. Commerce Department's highest rating award; William Bettendorf, who created the Bettendorf truck; country singer Suzy Bogguss; guitarist Jesse Johnson from the band Time (also known as Morris Day & The Time, the band was featured in Prince's movie *Purple Rain*); and former Chicago Cubs manager Joe Maddon, who guided the team to a World Series title in 2016, their first title in more than one hundred years, and who started his baseball career as a catcher for the Quad-City Angels.

There is no one beginning to the story of the Quad Cities region. Towns and settlements began to spring up across Illinois as European settlers continually pushed westward, hungry for new lands and opportunity.

As was the case in so many places, interactions with the Native American inhabitants, namely the Sauk and Meskwaki tribes, were often mixed. By 1832, the overall relations had broken down to the point of open warfare with the short-lived Black Hawk War. This resulted in the signing of the Black Hawk Treaty on the bluffs overlooking the Mississippi River and the forcible removal of both tribes.

A few years later, the town of Stephenson was founded, later renamed Rock Island. Davenport was founded soon after. As these cities grew and expanded, new towns were founded in the surrounding countryside, taking advantage of the rich soil of the region. In 1856, the first railroad bridge was built across the Mississippi River, connecting the region to the much larger markets of eastern cities. Businesses and factories grew up and prospered, as did the farmers in the rural areas.

By the turn of the century, the farmland of Iowa and Illinois had been established as some of the richest in the world. Ventures such as the Bettendorf Company were doing business on an international scale.

While the towns and cities of the region had their own beginnings, today they are interconnected by not only commerce but also a shared history of mutual prosperity and success. Sometimes, parts of that history still interact with us in the present.

All of this makes up the Quad Cities. The area has a rich, but also eerie, history.

Acknowledgements

FROM MICHAEL MCCARTY:
My lovely wife, Cindy McCarty; my blood brother John Brassard Jr.; The Amazing Kreskin; Bruce Walters; Jo Ann Brown; Scott Faust; Chef Steph; Kristin DeMarr; the McCartys; the Hultings; the Leonards; Mel Piff; Jack; Camilla; Holly; Brian; Quinn; Izzy; Bruce Cook; the memory of my parents, Bev and Gerald; and all my family and friends and fans—you are the reason I keep writing.

FROM JOHN BRASSARD JR.:
My wife, Elaine; my children; my parents, John Sr. and Tammy; my partner, Mike McCarty, for inviting me to do this with him; all the members of the Scott County Historical Society at Summit Church; the Scott County Historic Preservation Society; the *North Scott Press*; the *DeWitt Observer*; and all of my fans and supporters who have helped make this possible.

FROM MIKE AND JOHN:
Thanks also to The History Press; Chad Rhoad; Bruce Walters; Doug Smith; "Davenport Iowa History" on Facebook; Beverly Trout; Mutual UFO Network, Iowa (MUFON); Richard Van Fossen; "Iowa UFO Sightings and Discussions" on Facebook; Richard-Sloane Special Collection of the Davenport Library; Rock Island Library; Julie and Victoria Armas;

Michael and Penni Steen; Skellington Manor; Rick and Kathy Lopez; Igor's Bistro; Minda Powers-Douglas; Bill Douglas; the Renwick Mansion; Sarah and Dane Moulton; Chris Schlichting; Lisa Vinar; Dan Vinar Furniture Store; Ray Congrove; Deb Kuntzi; the Friends of Hauberg Civic Center Foundation; Cassie Steffen; Nick Simon; the Broadway Paranormal Society; Ariel Young; the Rock Island Paranormal; Mark Manuel; Q106.5 FM; Kai Swanson; J. Douglas Miller; Jordan Yaley; Ron Stewart; Samantha and Donald Goering; Jason Hess; Rachael Mullins Steiner; the Putnam Museum; the Source Bookstore; the Book Rack; Barnes & Noble; the Dark Side of Davenport Tours; The Amazing Kreskin; the Quad Cities Convention & Visitors Bureau; the Midwest Writing Center; the German American Heritage Center; Augustana College; Scott Community College; Joan Mauch; Jonathan Turner; Chad Lewis; Spellbound New Age & Gift Shop; Nick Vulich; Mary Angela Douglas; Rita Brandon; the *Quad-City Times*; the *Rock Island Argus*; the *Moline Dispatch*; *Paula Sands Live*; *Living Local*; Brittany Price; WHBF; KWQC; Quad Cities Chamber of Commerce; the people of the Quad Cities for being so supportive of our work; and, of course, Benjamin Gibson, our fearless acquisitions editor, who guided us through the winding course of getting this book published.

PART I

GHOSTS AND HAUNTED PLACES

Abandoned and Haunted

Grandview Terrace

For more than eighty years, the Royal Neighbors of America National Home, also known as the Grandview Terrace, stood high on the bluffs at 4760 Rockingham Road, Davenport, Iowa, overlooking the Mississippi River. A beacon for the West End was torn down in 2018.

More than five hundred people gathered for the dedication of the Royal Neighbors National Home on July 18, 1931. It fulfilled a resolution the society passed two years earlier to create a place where "the comforts of home could be provided for helpless mothers and other deserving members of our Society alone in the world and in need of such a service."

Built in Georgian Revival style by the Davenport architectural firm of Clausen, Kruse and Klein, the building was three stories high, built of red brick and had columned porches that extended the front of the building. Inside, there were floor-to-ceiling windows and a fireplace—31,061 square feet for the fifty-two residents.

In order to be accepted to live at the Royal Neighbors of America National Home, the resident had to turn over his or her assets to the society and, in turn, would be allowed to live at the home until he or she passed away. In 1993, the facility changed its name to the Grand Terrace.

Said Doug Smith, Quad City historian and the author of the book *Davenport*:

"A Real Home at the End of the Road," the Royal Neighbors of America National Home was maintained by Royal Neighbors of America, a fraternal beneficiary society, for the benefit of aged, deserving members without means of financial support or relatives to provide for them. Royal Neighbors of

America was founded in 1895 by nine women to empower women to better their lives through financial protection solutions and opportunities to give back to their communities. It stood firmly behind the women's suffrage movement and was one of the first fraternal societies to insure children and to insure women at a lower rate than men due to their mortality. Though organized in Iowa, they decided to incorporate in the State of Illinois, which had the most practicable insurance laws. After all state requirements were fulfilled, Royal Neighbors was chartered as a fraternal benefit society on March 21, 1895. The first home office was located in Peoria, but was moved to Rock Island in 1908. In February of 1930, the company purchased 40 acres in West Davenport on which to build their home for the aged. Over the years the property grew to encompass 77 acres. Faced with ever increasing costs, the facility finally closed in 2004 and was sold in 2006. As of 2015 the buildings are vacant and in a dilapidated condition.

In March 2012, the former retirement home was foreclosed on for nonpayment by Wells Fargo Bank, which held the mortgage, according to a representative of the Scott County Sheriff's Office. Wells Fargo declined comment on its plans for the property, and in 2018, the facility was torn down and the land put up for sale.

The Royal Neighbors of America National Home, also known as the Grandview Terrace, stood high on the bluffs at 4760 Rockingham Road, Davenport, Iowa. It was torn down in 2018. *Postcard from* Davenport Iowa History *(Doug Smith).*

Royal Neighbors of America National Home sign. *Photo by Michael McCarty.*

This story doesn't end with the Royal Neighbors of America National Home being abandoned and later torn down. There was more strange stuff that happened in between.

Julie Armas of Davenport was a home help aide and had visited the Grandview Terrace several times to assist the residents. When the place was abandoned, she also went to the former nursing home about a dozen times, sometimes with her daughter, Victoria, and son, Tony. "The first time we went," she said, "it wasn't hardly damaged at all. There were some windows which were in place. None of the bathrooms were destroyed, there wasn't that much graffiti."

Julie took more than fifty photos of the place that showed broken windows, graffiti, gang symbols, satanic drawings and damaged property. "The next time we went there, a month later on August 2015, it had been totally vandalized with graffiti, there was only one bathroom that wasn't messed with—the rest of the bathrooms were totally destroyed."

She continued, "That first time, we kept hearing this door closing by itself. But we ended up debunking that one, because the wind kept blowing, rocking the door back and forth."

However, there were a lot of other experiences, unexplained. The Armases felt a lot of negative energy in an area of the basement at the Grandview Terrace. "We didn't get any pictures of it because it was too dark. It was all these huge cages….It felt really creepy."

"That was weird," Victoria added. "It just felt bad down there. They got worse when you stepped inside the cages. When you were looking at them, they were bad, but when you went inside, you couldn't breathe—you just had to get out. It was really oppressive."

The Grandview Terrace after being abandoned. It has been heavily vandalized with broken windows and graffiti. *Photo by Julie Armas.*

One of the ghosts from the former nursing home followed the Armases back to her house. "In the kitchen, there were old receipts that were all over the floor. There was a receipt I picked up because I thought it looked good and brought it home with me. Victoria found somebody's blanket; it had been sealed around in plastic wrap, like you get when you take clothes to the laundry. It had a name sticker on it, so it belonged to somebody. We think somebody was attached to that blanket," Julie said. "The next morning, I was making coffee, and out of my peripheral vision, someone moved next to me. I was only one up at three o'clock in the morning. I looked and there was an old woman standing there, and she was angry. I jumped back, and she rushed me....I was totally shook up after that."

Her daughter also had an experience. "The night before that morning," Victoria stated. "I was in my bedroom sleeping. I woke up to a really heavy feeling, and I didn't like it. I went to turn over, there was this woman at the end of my bed; she was angry and dark. She just stood there, and I put the covers over my head and kept saying 'Just go to sleep, just go to sleep.'"

The next day, Victoria told her mother about it. "[Victoria] described the woman, and I said, 'That's the same woman.' We think we brought her home with the blanket," Julie commented. This happened the day after the mother and daughter went into Grandview Terrace.

Eventually, everything stopped when the blanket was removed. "The blanket was in my Grand Prix," Victoria remembered. "I think it was inside when I sold my car, it is with whoever has that car now."

THE BROADWAY PARANORMAL SOCIETY had several investigations of Grandview Terrace before it was leveled in 2018. Founder Cassie Steffen, who for the last eighteen years has worked as a demolition supervisor, received permission to explore the abandoned building:

> *We went to Grandview Terrace over twenty times. We were doing it the same time we were doing St. Luke's Hospital. We were going back and forth between St. Luke's and the Grandview Terrace. Unfortunately, that building came up for demolition at the same time St. Luke's came up. We split our time between both Grandview Terrace and St. Luke's Hospital… but St. Luke's was a lot more active.*
>
> *There was the spirit of a maintenance guy that stayed in the basement, mainly the boiler room. And we talked to him all the time.*
>
> *There was some kind of portal in the hallway coming out of the boiler room. And one of the members, who is also a medium, felt that people were coming and going out of that portal all the time. Our K2s* [a K2 meter is a tool for detecting spikes in electromagnetic energy] *were always going crazy right there. We were getting a lot of activity on our devices. We had a lot of EVPs* [Electronic Voice Phenomena] *down there—just random voices.*

Steffen continued:

> *One night, we had a large group there—it was kind of the same thing that happened at St. Luke's. We were downstairs,* [and] *we'd hear a door slam upstairs. When we'd go upstairs, we'd hear the door slam downstairs. One of our members said, "Stop!" As soon as he said that, the next door from where we were standing slams—scared everybody, most of them took off, running down the other hall.*
>
> *We heard the sound of breaking glass. We heard glass breaking a lot and no one was around, especially if we were in the basement. There was a walkout in the boiler room, and we heard breaking glass hitting the payment outside…we'd go outside and nobody was around.*
>
> *We kept hearing footsteps on the stairs. And that* [was] *followed by footsteps coming up and down the hall.*

Memorial to deceased members covered in vines. *Photo by Julie Armas.*

The staircase where both Victoria Armas and members of the Broadway Paranormal Society heard mysterious footsteps. *Photo by Julie Armas.*

Julie's daughter Victoria also heard unexplained footsteps—these same kind of phantom footsteps heard when Victoria and Tony explored the Royal Neighbors of America National Home without their mother.

"We kept hearing these mysterious footsteps. We couldn't get to them," Victoria recalled. "No matter where we were, it was always around us but we couldn't find it. The closer we got, we'd hear them, they'd be next to us—there was nothing. We were expecting to find some homeless people or something. This was in the basement, on the main level, on all the floors. This went through the whole building. It was like we were chasing someone, but there was no one around—it was always a few steps ahead."

Ariel Renee Young of Rock Island Paranormal has a theory about why Grandview Terrace might have had so much activity there. "Not too far away from the place, you have the Mississippi River. You can even see the river from it. The Mississippi River is a conductor—it has a lot of energy and spiritual activity associated with it."

Fairmount Cemetery

Fairmount Cemetery is located at 3902 Rockingham Road in Davenport, Iowa. Although it isn't the oldest graveyard in the city of Davenport, Iowa, it still has a long and illustrious history.

It started as the West Davenport Cemetery in 1881 and was located on the high bluffs overlooking the Mississippi River Valley west of the city. That same year, a thirty-three-year-old carpenter named John Dibbern became the first person interred there. The beautiful, peaceful scenery made it a lovely place to be buried in, and soon several others joined the young carpenter there.

In the late nineteenth century, cremation was not an acceptable method of handling the remains of the deceased, mostly due to a combination of social and religious reasons. However, a movement favoring cremation gradually gained momentum in Europe, especially Germany. It was only a matter of time before it spread to the United States.

The Northwestern Cremation Society, later renamed the Davenport Cremation Society, was soon established. One of its first orders of business was to construct a crematorium to serve the needs of the Quad City area. After some failed attempts to establish a facility in the downtown Davenport area, it finally gained permission to build at the West Davenport Cemetery.

The society sold stock to raise funds and, in 1889, commissioned prominent local architect Frederick G. Clausen to design its crematorium. In 1891, after a long, hard road, it was finally built.

Fairmount Cemetery, located at 3902 Rockingham Road in Davenport, Iowa. It was established in the West End of Davenport in 1881. *Photo by Michael McCarty.*

The crematorium at West Davenport Cemetery was only the second one built west of the Mississippi River. It was an elegant brick building, containing colorful stained-glass windows and was surrounded by well-maintained grounds. A flight of stairs ascended to a set of double doors that led into a large central room that served as a chapel.

Initially, the crematorium served not only the city of Davenport but also the needs of the state of Iowa and larger cities such as Chicago, Minneapolis, Omaha and Denver. In its first ten years, it performed 133 cremations; by the mid-1980s, it was handling 6,000, and by 2014, that number had grown to 11,700 cremations. Several hundred people would eventually be cremated here, including such notables as L.P. Best, a prominent Davenport businessman.

In 1900, the board of the West Davenport Cemetery decided to change the name of the cemetery. Instead of just choosing for themselves, the board members decided to make it more democratic and made the selection process into a contest. The person to come up with the chosen name would win a free burial spot in the cemetery. After some time and deliberation, the winner was the name that the cemetery is known by today: Fairmount.

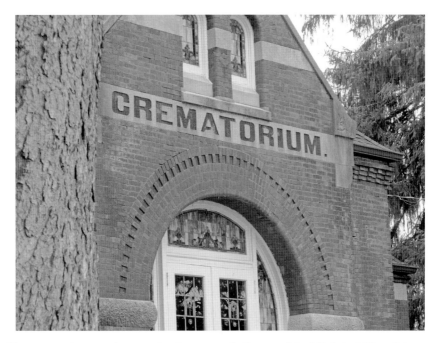

The crematorium was the second such structure built west of the Mississippi River. It is an elegant brick building, containing colorful stained-glass windows. *Photo by Michael McCarty.*

In 1927, the Fairmount Cemetery Board decided to look into building a community mausoleum. While individual or family mausoleums can be found in several large cemeteries across the country, a community mausoleum provides a beautiful, clean place to inter your loved ones without burdening families with the cost or effort of annual upkeep.

The public loved the idea, and construction began in 1928. Situated with a commanding view from the top of the river bluffs, the building was made from concrete with a stone and marble exterior. Inside, electric lighting illuminated marble floors and spacious walkways, while stained-glass windows added a reverential effect.

By March of the following year, the Fairmount Cemetery Mausoleum had been completed, and the general public was invited to view it. Today, the mausoleum is still there, carrying on its eternal vigil from the bluffs above the Mississippi. The crematory is also there, standing with the distinction of being the ninth-oldest crematory in the United States.

Having been around for so long, it should come as no surprise that Fairmount Cemetery has more than its share of stories. One of these is the legend of the Thirteen Steps.

Local legend claims that if you count your steps when climbing up a particular set of stairs near the crematorium, you will count a different number of steps on the way down. The authors couldn't help themselves and decided to test the legend for themselves. Unfortunately for the story, they came up with the same number of steps up and down.

"We did that too," said Ariel Renee Young of Rock Island Paranormal. "[We] came up with the exact going number up and coming down." Formed in 2006, Rock Island Paranormal is a group that seeks to investigate paranormal phenomena and to help individuals with any supernatural experiences that they are unsure how to handle on their own. Beginning in September 2016, the group has conducted several investigations at the cemetery.

"The mausoleums always have some kind of readings or activity," Young said. "Every time you go there, you can hear footsteps. You'll walk up, and if there are only two of you there, it can get kind of creepy—you are looking and there is nobody moving…you hear the footsteps walking around or you hear the leaves brushing and there is no wind and no one else around, yet you hear the footsteps walking and the leaves crunching."

At other times, Young claims, she and her fellow investigators could distinctly hear people talking on the grounds, even though there was no one there. "Sometimes you will hear disembodied voices, and they echo, especially since it is like a canyon-like area. My cousin lived next to the cemetery, and he heard numerous children's voices."

Young has also had a frightening experience at the cemetery involving shadows. "At night, it is spooky. This wasn't even an investigation. I was helping my cousin find his dog that got loose that night. The dog ran through the cemetery. I saw this big shadow—it had to be seven feet tall. I turned around, thinking the shadow must have been cast by my cousin, because he is a bigger guy and I thought he was behind me. I turned around and it just vanished."

While cemeteries the world over are the final resting places of our loved ones, not all of them are haunted. If this is the case, what could possibly be causing the phenomena that have been experienced in and around Fairmount?

Ariel Renee Young believes that incidents of vandalism that have occurred at the cemetery over the years might have contributed to all the ethereal occurrences. For several years, Fairmount was well outside the boundaries of the Davenport city limits. Even now, after decades of urban growth, the cemetery sits on the outskirts of the city. Much of it is hidden by trees and

A mausoleum near where the others were broken into and vandalized. *Photo by Bruce Walters.*

steep ravines as well, lending camouflage to any nocturnal activities that some individuals chose to engage in.

Being there conveys a feeling of isolation, even on the edges of the grounds, where well-developed neighborhoods of houses have long been established. It might have been this sense of remoteness that encouraged a young man named Richard Edwards to break into several crypts there in 1977. In at least one crypt, Edwards destroyed a casket and then pulled out the body. He also stole a human skull. Police arrested him for his crimes, and the crypts were resealed.

Twenty years later, the crypts were broken into again. This time, no suspect was ever found. Richard Kronfeld, who was the cemetery superintendent of Fairmount at the time, believed that the robbery was linked to Satanists because the bodies were ransacked, and it was quite possible that they took some bones with them. The robbery took place during a full moon, which might have further coincided with occult activity.

Kronfeld also believed that these break-ins were related to an earlier theft that had taken place a short time before, when a power saw was taken from Fairmount's main mausoleum.

Illustration by Jason McLean.

In the fall of 2008, the crypts were broken into yet again, although this time was by far the most disturbing. Body parts were thrown around the interiors and, in at least one instance, rearranged. One police officer even stated that it felt like there was something else going on with the break-in outside of a simple act of vandalism or robbery.

"There is no doubt in my mind, there is a lot of activity around the mausoleums," Ariel Young stated.

Young's cousin, who lived nearby, had a particularly strange experience during a house fire:

> *They lived at the bottom of the hill at the cemetery. Next door to the crematorium there was a house there, and it caught on fire three or four years ago. The only reason his children made it out, something—they don't know what—was holding the door shut so the smoke wouldn't get into the girls' bedroom.*
>
> *There are hand prints, clear as day, holding the door, and there is smoke all around it. He said, "I had to force open that door to get my girls out, because it was being held shut. There was no lock on the door." He is a big*

*guy, and with all of his bang and push with all of his strength to knock
that door open, to get inside of his daughters' room.*

[My cousin] *said, "If* [the unidentified force] *wasn't holding
the door closed, that smoke would have gotten to the girls and would have
caused a lot of smoke inhalation." He was glad that something helped him.*

Today, Fairmount Cemetery is the final resting place of thousands of
Quad Citians who built their lives in the region. Perhaps, and for their own
reasons, some of them continue to linger and interact with the living.

The Freemasons of the Quad Cities

The Masonic Temples are buildings for the Freemasons, who belong to an organization whose roots go back to the guilds of stonemasons that built cathedrals during England's Middle Ages. The Masons organized in the seventeen and eighteenth centuries to teach members their trade, as well as to impart moral guidance. As the demand for construction decreased, the guilds began to accept non-stonemasons as members. Today, Masons use ancient rites and trappings to promote brotherly love, relief and truth, using allegory and tools of the old stonemasons.

Masonic organizations were not strictly for men. They have orders for other family members, including Eastern Star for women, DeMolay and Builders for boys and Job's Daughters and Rainbow for girls, according to the Rock Island Preservation Society and an article written by Diane Oestreich for the *Rock Island Argus*.

DAVENPORT, IOWA: THE OLD MASONIC TEMPLE

Sitting majestically just south of Central High School, the old Masonic Temple's history runs as deep as the foundations beneath it.

In the early years of the twentieth century, local Masonic leaders had an idea. At the time, all four of the Quad Cities were experiencing a kind of golden age of growth and prosperity. They had grown from frontier and

The Old Masonic Temple, Lodge No. 39, now Lyceum Hall at Palmer College of Chiropractic. Built in 1922, this building is located on Seventh Street and Brady Street in Davenport, Iowa. *Photo by Bruce Walters.*

farm towns into bustling cities, ready and eager to spring onto a bigger stage. The Freemasons wanted not only to be a part of that but also to help it along. They envisioned a venue that could accommodate statewide and even national Masonic events, hosting hundreds of people. The Masons were also aware that no one in the area at that time had a place to host such large-scale events.

In 1915, the fraternity decided that the site between Main and Brady Streets would be ideal for its purpose and bought the property. Four years later, the Masons moved into the next phase of the project. A special committee, named the New Masonic Temple Association, was formed for the express purpose of making their new building a reality.

Wanting to make its new building the best it could be, the association began to undertake in-depth research in order to meet the needs of the order. This included not only being able to accommodate its present membership but also planning ahead for future growth. The association toured the nation and looked at several new Masonic Temples being built at the time, adapting its favorite design ideas from each location.

Finally, in the summer of 1921, it was ready to begin. The association used all local companies for its project, from the architects to the finished carpentry. From 1921 to 1923, home-grown workers constructed a three-story stone-faced giant. It cost them about $1 million, or nearly $15,206,000 today.

The New Temple included offices, lodge rooms, a reading room, restrooms and an apartment for the custodian. A 1,200-seat grand banquet hall was located in the basement, and a 3,000-seat auditorium was located on the uppermost floor.

From early on, the Masons were keen on supporting their community by allowing the temple to be used as a public venue. On October 21, 1923, Anna Pavlova and the Ballets Russes became the first act to entertain audiences at the Masonic Temple, but they would be far from the last. Over the following decades, world-famous entertainers appeared here, such as Simon and Garfunkel, Wayne Newton, the Carpenters, Barry Manilow, Merle Haggard, Johnny Cash, Journey, Styx, Ted Nugent, the Turtles and the Beach Boys. In 1980, Michael McCarty even saw George Carlin do his stand-up comedy there and met the comedian backstage after the show.

Door entrance at the Old Masonic Temple that reads "Masonic Temple Let There Be Light." *Photo by Bruce Walters.*

In 1995, the Masonic Temple was sold to Palmer College of Chiropractic. In the years following, it was used for various purposes, including as a museum. A former employee who wished to remain anonymous stated that a time capsule was also found at the Masonic Temple when Palmer College took over, but they don't know the fate of the container.

Over the decades, strange stories have trickled out of the building. Some individuals have claimed that they heard voices coming from a room, obviously deep in conversation. As they're about to enter the room, they open their mouths to say something...only to see that there's no one in there.

Others have allegedly heard phantom footsteps or been touched by invisible hands. Objects have reportedly been seen moving by themselves. Some even say that they saw apparitions within the long hallways of the building.

Since 1923, thousands of people have passed in and out of the old Masonic Temple. For many Freemasons, it was a central part of their lives. Other people might have seen the best concert of their lives there or met someone in a class that changed their view of the world. If they have since passed on, then it would be easy to imagine that their spirit, still remembering that one key place, that key moment, would be drawn back to that place.

The old Masonic Temple was built to serve not only the many members of the order but also the entire Quad City community. Today, perhaps, the building serves the needs of the living as well as the dead.

Rock Island, Illinois: Skellington Manor

The Skellington Manor, located at 420 Eighteenth Street in Rock Island, had been a Masonic Temple for ninety-five years, until it was sold to Michael and Penni Steen, who ran the popular Halloween attraction Terror in the Woods in Donahue, Iowa.

The former Masonic Temple cost $75,000 to construct and was built in 1913. The building covers more than twenty-eight thousand square feet and has a basement, a main level, two mezzanines (floors between floors, like a half floor) and third and fourth floors (typically where an attic would be).

When Terror in the Woods closed in 2007, "We were looking for another venue to do a haunted house. The Masonic Temple in Rock Island was viable—it was sitting nearly empty," said Penni Steen. "With all its nooks and crannies, basement and attic, even a stage with lights that still worked, it was a great location for another haunted house."

Steen continued, "The Freemasons had thirteen different orders, but the biggest was the Trio." [No. 57 Lodge, Ancient Free and Accepted Mason Commandery; No. 18 Knights Templar, Lodge 658; and Royal Arch Mason—the trio group was the oldest organization in the area from 1848, and its name refers to the three towns of Rock Island, Moline and Camden Mills, which later became Milan, Illinois.] The Masonic Temple was the hub of the community with its many banquets and events." The Steens decided that their new purchase would not only be great for a haunted house but could also be utilized year-round for wedding receptions, formal functions and gatherings. They named the building Skellington Manor in honor of the character Jack Skellington, the king of Halloween Town in *The Nightmare Before Christmas*.

The Steens spent four months renovating Skellington Manor. A short while after that, a group of Freemasons came to remove a time capsule that had been placed in the corner of the building when it was erected. Unfortunately, the capsule was too far into the foundation, and they were unable to retrieve it.

The awning of Skellington Manor. *Photo by Michael McCarty.*

The Steens decided to create their own time capsule, filled with newspaper clippings about their Terror in the Woods venue, plus some articles about President Barack Obama being the first African American president. "My husband wanted to put in some CDs, but they might not even have CD players around in one hundred years," she said.

Skellington Manor became a huge local hit for both public and private functions. Their annual Halloween attraction, Terror at Skellington Manor, became the top haunted attraction in the Quad Cities. During other parts of the year, they host escape rooms and the murder-mystery dinner theater *It's a Mystery*. "Our real estate agent, Jerry Wolking, was in *It's a Mystery*, that is how that came about," Ms. Steen said.

Skellington Manor has been investigated by ten local paranormal groups, including Rock Island Paranormal. "Mostly they've gotten EVPs around the Masonic artifacts here and there," Steen explained.

Rock Island Paranormal (RIP) was formed in 2006 to help homes and businesses. It did its first investigation at the Manor in 2011. "And we were the group to give them the okay it was haunted," said Ariel Renee Young, a member of RIP. "They turned it into a haunted house, and before that, it was a Masonic Temple. With the Masonic Temples, a lot of times, women weren't allowed in certain areas. When we, being women, went into those areas, we'd get a lot of readings on the K2s. We had several EVPs basically saying, 'You don't belong here, you get out.'"

"When I was in there in 2003, I kind of felt that in certain areas for me, it wasn't so much that it was unwelcome, but rather that it was private," John Brassard Jr. recalled. "Like being in someone's bedroom uninvited."

Rock Island Paranormal members didn't feel like they were getting negative energy. "There were some times I was a little creeped out," Young said, "but I wouldn't call it negative energy. We had more evidence with disembodied voices, people saying certain things. Once we got a really creepy laugh. I made a silly joke, and none of the other members laughed. Then we got this really weird really eerie laughter when we went back over the evidence."

Young continued, "People have been touched or poked or even pushed when they are working in their scare spot during the haunted house."

Steen added, "We had a couple of haunted house actors that reported they were touched."

"We didn't get much in the attic," Young said, "or in the basement. We got a lot more activity where people walk around during the haunted house attraction they do during the fall—that conducts energy as well. We also saw a shadow walk by the door when nobody was around." Young said.

Skellington Manor, located at 420 Eighteenth Street in Rock Island, was a Masonic Temple (no. 658) for ninety-five years. *Photo by Michael McCarty.*

"I've gotten chills and creepy feelings here and there," Steen said. "My husband was even poked and couldn't explain it. But I'm not really frightened by it. I think the ghosts and us can cohabitate together. They aren't harmful."

"Years ago, I had a great opportunity to go to Skellington Manor," said Jason Hess, author of the book *So You Still Want to Be a Ghost Hunter?* "To be honest, anyone could go there during the month of October. See, it is a haunt—a haunted house that is open for the month—and to be honest, it's a great show. The owners still have the lodge books and some cool artifacts."

According to Hess, he originally went to Skellington Manor to see if the building was actually haunted. "The building itself is huge, with a lot of ground to cover during an investigation. Complicating this was the fact that the Terror at Skellington Manor attraction is kept up year-round....It's a huge maze where we had members of our paranormal team get confused and couldn't find where they were going."

Whatever the problems, the team enjoyed investigating Skellington Manor and returned multiple times. One of these visits was featured on a local morning television program. "We chased voices, saw shadows moving, and captured a lot of evidence," said Hess.

One of the tools that they used was a full-spectrum camera, which picks up spectrums of light that are invisible to the human eye. In one of the photos taken with it (one that was featured on the show), a face can clearly be seen within arms' reach of the team.

Hess claimed that team members distinctly heard voices in the building. When they went to investigate, they found nothing there. A few seconds later, the same voice spoke again, this time directly behind them. "There was a time we heard a voice and went around the corner to come face to face with one of the props," he said.

Hess's favorite story from Skellington Manor comes from an incident where he and his team were walking along some old lockers in the building. All of the locker doors were closed, and the room was quiet.

The team decided to conduct an EVP session to see if they could speak to the spirits alleged to be in the building. They did everything they could think of to get a response, including provoking them, a technique used by ghost hunters in which they challenge the spirits in the hope of making them angry enough to show some kind of response.

When nothing happened, the team decided to move on to the next part of the building. They went only a short distance when they all distinctly heard a locker door slam closed. Shocked, they turned around and went back. Using flashlights, the team thoroughly investigated the area but couldn't find anything. "It was such a great place for history, a Halloween haunt and a true haunted building," Mr. Hess said.

The Steens take a philosophical approach to the phenomena. "I feel we leave our energy footprint when we pass," Penni Steen said. "That energy might still remain and might get stirred up a little when we do the haunted house in the fall."

For nearly one hundred years, the Masonic Hall was a focal point of life for local Freemasons. Their members were taught to practice goodwill and virtue there, reaching out and helping the community. Even though the building has changed hands, perhaps some of the Freemasons remain, still involved in the activities that they had loved so much in life.

BETTENDORF, IOWA: W.P. BETTENDORF MANSION

The former W.P. Bettendorf Mansion stands majestically on the river bluff overlooking the Mississippi River Valley below, a mute testimony to the power and glory of a bygone age. Initially the dream of a successful businessman, the home would eventually become known as the home of the Iowa Masonic Nursing Facility.

Referred to by some as the best-kept secret of the Quad Cities, the story of the beautiful former mansion is tinged with tragic loss, sudden death and even madness. Does it come as any surprise that some claim that a few of the former owners may still reside there, years after their passing?

The mansion was the vision of William Peter Bettendorf, an ultra-successful inventor and industrialist, and was built at 2500 Grant Street no. 1, Bettendorf, Iowa. In 1909, he was doing business with some of the wealthiest and most powerful businessmen and industrialists in the nation. This wasn't a clientele that impressed easily, and William knew that it was going to take something spectacular to show them that he was the kind of successful manufacturer they would want to make deals with.

The mansion, formerly known as the Iowa Masonic Nursing Facility, located at 2500 Grant Street no. 1, Bettendorf, Iowa. It was the vision of William Bettendorf, a successful inventor and industrialist and one of the founders of Bettendorf, Iowa. *Photo by John Brassard Jr.*

It went without saying that the house was going to have to be opulent, on a par with other midwestern mansions in Chicago and St. Louis. It had to have elaborate plaster moldings, woodwork and, of course, furniture. But William wanted something more. His plan was to give a tour of his factory to clients during the day, showing them how streamlined and efficient his best-selling products were. Afterward, they and their families would be brought to his home on the river bluff overlooking his operations.

Throughout the rest of the evening, his guests would be surrounded by all of the opulence that his substantial fortune could muster. At the conclusion of the evening, they would be taken to their accommodations upstairs.

The rooms were divided up into suites, each with a bedroom, bathroom and sitting room. It would be like a small home away from home for his guests, allowing them to feel perfectly comfortable while affording them all the privacy they could want.

It was an unusual design for a home, but William hadn't achieved such great success by being conventional. Never one to simply leave the work to others, he commissioned a nine-room bungalow to be built close to where the mansion was being constructed. From there, he oversaw the day-to-day operations of both his new home and his factory down below.

The mansion was three stories tall, boasted more than twenty rooms and was surrounded by elaborately landscaped gardens. The exterior was done in the Spanish-influenced New Mission style that was popular that time in the southwestern United States. It also allowed the home to stand out that much more.

The interior, in sharp contrast to the exterior, was built in a heavily European style, namely Bavarian. It was full of rich, dark mahogany, polished English oak and elaborate plasterwork. It was to be decorated with furniture, paintings and other items picked out by William on trips to Europe.

He hired European master craftsmen to come to America and handle the elaborate decorative woodwork. The grounds around the house were covered with well-manicured decorative gardens. It was filled with electrical lighting and even outlets, an unusual feature for that time, powered by his company's power plant nearby.

William's journey wasn't always an easy one. William's two young children died a short time apart during a diphtheria epidemic that burned through Davenport in the early 1890s. In 1901, Mary, his wife of more than twenty years, fell ill and passed away after visiting her parents in Illinois.

The following year, William and his brother and business partner, Joseph, almost lost their entire operation. Two devastating fires only a few months apart nearly destroyed their entire factory in Davenport. This prompted their move to nearby Gilbert, just east of Davenport.

Things thankfully turned around for them from then on. They were able to rebuild the company and even expand it. The brothers invested heavily in the town, and the grateful citizens renamed their town Bettendorf in their honor.

In 1908, William met and married Elizabeth Staby, a department head at the J.M.H. Peterson and Sons department store in Davenport.

As a hands-on employer, William used the newly built bungalow a short distance away from where the mansion was being built to oversee the process. It also served as a home for himself, his new bride and his parents until the home was finally finished.

There was very little that could have made William's life any better. Then, in 1910, William got sick when he was on vacation with his family at Lake Okoboji in western Iowa. Cutting their vacation short, they immediately returned home. The doctor who examined William determined that he had food poisoning and that his sickness would pass in a few days. Sure enough, the symptoms passed, and William started to get ready to go back to work at the factory. As he did, however, William suddenly fainted and fell to the floor one day.

There was something seriously wrong, and everyone knew it. Joseph Bettendorf sent for a specialist from Chicago to examine his older brother. The specialist didn't give a favorable diagnosis. He informed them that William had a perforated bowel and that he needed emergency surgery as soon as possible. However, he also said that the patient had only a 1 percent chance of surviving the procedure.

With little choice, William consented to the operation. A makeshift operating theater was prepared in the kitchen (or the dining room, depending on the source) of the bungalow, using electric lighting powered by the company power plant.

Unfortunately, William couldn't beat the odds and died on the table. He was only fifty-three years old. Elizabeth inherited one-third of his immense wealth, including the home and surrounding property. The mansion became her home for the next twelve years.

While Elizabeth was very socially active, hosting card parties and the like at the home for her friends, she performed many of her more benevolent activities very quietly. After being abandoned by her first husband, Elizabeth had been forced to raise their son, Oscar, mostly by herself, with help from her ex-husband's parents. She knew what it was like to be a young woman in difficult circumstances and was determined to use her fortune to help young women such as herself. Elizabeth went so far as to give them rides home to make sure they got where they were going safely, sometimes even taking in some of them on a short-term basis at the mansion. She did all of this without telling anyone, and when Elizabeth died in 1922, her family was told about it for the first time.

Elizabeth's son, Oscar Staby, was an only child and sole heir to her fortune. For two years, he maintained the mansion. During those years, the Iowa Freemasons were looking for a property that they could use as a nursing and care facility for their members and their families. They needed something large and well kept, and although they had looked at a few properties around the state, they still hadn't found anything.

Oscar was a devoted Mason himself and had heard about their plan. He contacted them, told them about the mansion and, in an act of amazing generosity, offered to sell the property to them for a mere $50,000, half the property's assessed value. It was exactly what was needed, and the Iowa Freemasons agreed to buy the property in 1924, officially finalizing the sale the following year.

Oscar turned over the keys and moved to Los Angeles with his family, where he was a successful businessman and investor. Two years later, in October 1927, the Stabys sat down to Sunday dinner without a care in the world. Everything was fine when, all of a sudden, Oscar's hands started to shake uncontrollably. He felt nervous, so nervous that he couldn't control himself. He quickly excused himself, dropping his knife and fork on the table. Without another word, Oscar walked quickly out of the room and went upstairs.

His wife and two daughters were shocked. Everything was so sudden and so strange. They had never seen Oscar act like that before and had no idea why he would now. As they sat there in confusion, the women heard the sharp report of gunshot from upstairs. Racing up the stairs, they found Oscar in the bathroom, dead. He had just shot himself in the head.

There was a short investigation, but no cause for Oscar's breakdown was ever discovered. There were no shady business dealings or covert affairs. The coroner ruled his death a suicide caused by temporary insanity, and Oscar was quietly buried at Forest Lawn Cemetery in Los Angeles, California.

Back in Bettendorf, the Masons built a large addition off the main mansion, with seventy beds to accommodate their membership and their families. The facility was a raving success, and the property continued to be developed over the following decades.

The mansion itself, used as administrative offices, was left virtually untouched over that time. While the majority of the furnishings were sold off, everything was very much as it was when Elizabeth Staby Bettendorf had resided there. Perhaps that is why, according to some, something *else* walked the old corridors.

One night, several years ago, Jo Smith (name changed for privacy) was in her office, working late. She was making good progress on the overflow that needed to be taken care of, and she figured that she could just grab something to eat on the way home.

"Jo!" a voice called. She looked over at the doorway from her computer screen. There was no one there, so the voice must have come from outside.

"Yeah?" Jo called back. No answer. Her co-worker, Sam Norton, was also working late that night. It had been a woman's voice calling Jo's name, so it must have been her. She sat, her ears straining against the quiet. Nothing. "It must have been my imagination," she thought as she began to type again. Jo smiled. Now that she was hearing voices, it was definitely time to call it a day.

"Jo!" the voice called again. This time, Jo *knew* that she had heard someone calling her name. Pushing her chair back, she stood up and walked out into the hallway.

"Yeah? I'm in my office. What do you need?" Jo called. Once again, no answer.

That was odd. Why wouldn't Sam, or whoever it was, answer? Curious, she walked down the short hallway and toward Sam's office. As she approached, Jo could see that the room was completely dark. A tingle of unease pulsed through Jo. She looked around into the other rooms but saw that they were dark as well. Just then, the door to the other part of the facility opened, and Sam stepped through.

Jo smiled. "Hi Sam. What did you need?" she asked.

Sam smiled back, looking slightly confused. "Uh, hi. What do you mean?"

Confused, Jo asked, "You were calling my name just a few minutes ago, but I couldn't find you."

Sam's smile faded. "You heard me calling your name?"

"Yes! Twice."

Sam looked hard at Jo. "Jo," she said. "I haven't been in here for at least half an hour. I don't know who was calling you, but it wasn't me."

Others had experiences as well. Some, like Jo, heard voices, while others unexplained noises. One evening, a worker was alone in one of the offices. They had one of the outside doors open, standing just inside while taking in the breathtaking view of the Mississippi River from the home.

Lost in the moment, they suddenly felt someone push them hard from behind, sending them stumbling out of the door. Spinning around to confront their attacker, they felt their blood run cold as they realized that there was no one there—they were still very much alone in the house.

Was the spirit of Elizabeth Staby Bettendorf wandering the house that she had called home for all of those years? Was it the ghost of her son, Oscar, struck down too soon in the throes of a sudden madness? Perhaps it was even William Bettendorf himself, enjoying the luxury of the mansion that he built but never got to live in.

Eventually, someone was able to obtain an old photograph of Elizabeth Staby Bettendorf. Framing it, they hung it in a place of honor in their office. Once the picture was hung, all of the activity seemed to stop.

In 2016, Iowa Masonic began to open the home for by-appointment tours and special events. Since then, the members have shared the history of the home and its former owners, shedding light into a long-forgotten corner of Quad Cities history.

Perhaps the ghosts that walked the home simply wanted to be remembered. Now that they are, perhaps they will rest more easily.

The Haunted Furniture Store

The massive, 49,600-square-foot building located at 500 Twentieth Street in Rock Island started life as the Rock Island YMCA. Built in 1912 by John and Susanne Hauberg, the YMCA was the center of the community. Not only did it host youth programs, but it also provided affordable sleeping rooms for out-of-town travelers on the third and fourth floors of the building. During wartime, soldiers were allowed to stay there for free if they showed up in uniform.

A fire in 1976 caused it to close a year later. In 1994, the Vinar family bought the building and moved their eighty-two-year-old furniture business there.

Over the years, some people started to notice that some odd things took place there. They talked about their experiences privately but rarely shared these stories with their customers. That all changed when Cassie Steffen of the Broadway Paranormal Society just happened to be there shopping for an end table.

While she was looking, Cassie started a conversation with Lisa Vinar, the owner. As they talked, she asked Lisa if she or her employees had ever had any strange experiences there. Lisa said that they happened all the time: "I was standing here next to my desk [by her office] and I heard footsteps. They sounded like someone wearing boots going down the stairs. I also heard someone cough in the stairwell....Another time, my son was working on his car in the garage. He heard someone walking up the ramp but didn't see anyone. He kept working on his car, and then the door at the top of the ramp opened and closed."

Dan Vinar Furniture Store, located at 500 Twentieth Street, Rock Island. Sunspots mysterious appeared when this photo was taken. *Photo by Bruce Walters.*

At the end of the conversation, Lisa gave Cassie her business card and permission to do what would be the first paranormal investigation of the building. It was one that she would remember well.

"The first night we were there, we just did a walk-through," Cassie said. "I heard voices talking, having a conversation. I was on the third floor [near] the elevator shaft; I could hear voices through the door going into the elevator shaft. I walked up there with another team member to open the door, to make out what they were saying. Nobody was there and it just stopped. It was done."

Several investigators and paranormal enthusiasts have been through the one-hundred-year-old furniture store since then. Their experiences range from the intriguing to the terrifying.

Minda Powers-Douglas, author of the book *Chippiannock Cemetery* (Images of America series), is among them. "The two times I've been there, I've experienced things," she said. "I felt the temperature shift on the fourth floor. It's where a lot of the activity is. The basement level where the pool used to be is also very active." The basement is the former site of an enormous fifty-thousand-gallon swimming pool. It was filled in several years ago and converted into storage space.

"While in the basement, I felt something brush against my calf and then my knee," said Powers-Douglas. "Across from me, something was pushing

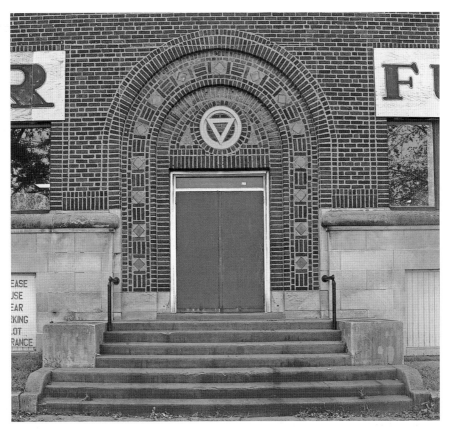

The former entrance of the Dan Vinar Furniture Store at Twentieth Street. *Photo by Bruce Walters.*

my mom away from the wall she was leaning against. We were with around fifteen people there, and others were experiencing things too."

During one of its subsequent investigations of the store, the Broadway Paranormal Society allegedly contacted a spirit haunting the area. "There was a little girl in the basement who would communicate with us a lot in the electrical room, where the old pool was," said Cassie Steffen.

"I haven't been able to confirm this one way or another, but a child supposedly drowned in the pool," said Nick Simon, one of the team's investigators. "I heard a child's voice while doing an investigation on the first floor, above where the pool once was, and it said, 'Boy, you are really tall!'"

Activity has also been reported on the second floor of the building, especially in what is now called the chair room. Originally, the room was a classroom used in the old YMCA. Paranormal investigator Jason Hess caught several orbs on camera there, and Cassie Steffen claims that her team communicated with the spirit of a former teacher there.

The Broadway Paranormal Society also reported strange activity in the former gymnasium. "In the gymnasium, there is a track up above. We've seen shadow figures moving around on the track, and they are staring at us. That is an active spot," said Steffen.

Perhaps the most active places in the building are on the third and fourth floors. "My hair was lifted up once on the fourth floor. I watched a piece of somebody's hair lift up, too, across the hallway from me. That was strange," said Powers-Douglas. "To actually have something physically done to you or see it done with your own eyes makes you rethink things."

Another experience she had involved her mother. "My mother and I went to a paranormal event at the furniture store a couple years ago. While we were on the third floor, we were shown into a room. The lady there asked for a volunteer, and my mom offered. She handed my mom a balloon to place on her hand. Then, to an unseen entity, she said, 'Can you knock the balloon out of this nice lady's hand?'" said Powers-Douglas.

"Mom kept her hand very still. I didn't see any movement on her part. Eventually, it started slowly rocking just a little. Then it looked like it was 'popcorning.' That's the best way I can describe it. It bounced a little on her hand like popcorn does when it's just starting to pop. Then it rolled off her hand and onto the floor. It was fantastic."

"I usually don't go into the sleeping rooms much," Lisa Vinar said. "On the fourth floor, I was mopping one night. Someone grabbed my rear end, and I told him to knock it off!"

While people have had experiences throughout the top floors, the trunk room on the second is especially active. This was a storage area where travelers could store their belongings, usually kept in trunks, until they were ready to leave. To make things easier for them, the room was located next to a freight elevator.

During one investigation, the Broadway Paranormal Society used a piece of equipment called an "Sbox" in the trunk room. The device allegedly picks up electronic voice phenomena of spirits and translates the sounds into word-generated radio waves, allowing the spirit to speak through it.

"When we did the Sbox at the trunk room, we had really dirty words coming through. We came to the conclusion that the men staying there would sneak some of their women up the elevator shaft so they wouldn't get caught and would go into the trunk room, because it was a very private room," Cassie Steffen said.

"Every once in a while, you'll be looking down the hallway," says Nick Simon, "[and] you'll see what looks like a shadow of someone leaning out of one of the rooms staring at you…[they] will go back in and lean out. One of my favorite things to do at this building is to see what shadows lean in or move around on the fourth floor."

But who could some of these spirits be? According to Nick Simon, five men died at the YMCA over the years, all of natural causes. However, Simon's research also uncovered one connection between the building and a Quad Cities murder that took place in 1969.

Twenty-year-old John Gregson Dickson was both a resident and employee of the YMCA. He had formerly worked at the Moline Elks Club but was eventually fired.

On July 26, 1969, John J. Jones, the bar manager of the Moline Elks Club, was stabbed to death when someone attempted to rob the facility. A very large size 52 coat was found at the scene of the crime. After an intensive investigation, the coat was traced back to the six-foot-three Dickson. He was arrested and eventually pleaded guilty to the murder.

Could the guilt and negative emotion felt by Dickson as he lived in the building have left a stain there that has somehow allowed it to be haunted?

Lisa Vinar has conducted her own investigations of her building. She has captured unusual phenomena on both recording and video devices. "The first day I got my recorder, I put it in the stairwell. [While] I was sweeping the stairs, you hear my mother say my name. Loud and clear. Another time, you hear a voice of a woman screaming, 'No, no! Help!' and then you hear a door slam," she said.

Her video footage is just as intriguing. "I used to set up cameras," Vinar said. "I would have these cat toys that would light up if you touched them. I was going to put one in the trunk room to have it on camera. I turned it on [the cat toy] and tried to set up the camera, [but] I was having issues with it, and you look down and the ball was lighting up."

"I built my own SOS camera," Ms. Vinar said. "I did catch in the chair room a figure that was sitting in the chair, and I got him to lift his arm above his head and wave at me. He also waved goodbye when I asked."

Although she has encountered several strange things over the years, Ms. Vinar remains in good spirits about all the paranormal activity. "They are just there, unless they want to be seen. They don't bother me and I don't bother them," she said. "They have been friendly toward me because my husband's here protecting me [her husband, Dan, passed away in 2013]. Plus, I've been in this building since 1994. They are used to me."

Hauberg Estate and the Ghosts of the Carriage House

T he Denkmann-Hauberg House, also known as the Hauberg Estate, is located at 1300 Twenty-Fourth Street, Rock Island, Illinois. It is a splendid, twenty-thousand-square-foot mansion surrounded by ten acres. An eight-thousand-square-foot carriage house nearby completes the property.

The Prairie-style dwelling was designed by Chicago architect Robert C. Spencer, a friend and officemate of Frank Lloyd Wright's. According to the *Highland Park Historical District History & Architect*, "The home two took years to construct, from 1909–1911 and was commissioned by heiress Susanne Denkmann. Her favorite flower—the tulip—is featured stylistically on all the exterior and interior. Spencer adapted the tulip to stone inserts, plaster molding, wood organ screens, fixtures, decorative title and much more."

Susanne Denkmann was the youngest daughter of Frederik Denkmann, founding partner in the Weyerhauser-Denkmann Lumber Company. In 1911, at the age of thirty-nine, she married a forty-one-year-old lawyer named John Hauberg.

John Hauberg was a well-regarded naturalist and founded the Black Hawk Hiking Club in 1920. He was instrumental in securing Black Hawk's Watch Tower as a state park in 1927, and much of his personal collection of Native American artifacts helped create the John Hauberg Museum of Native American Life.

In 1956, John and Susanne's children donated the home to the City of Rock Island to be used as the Hauberg Civic Center. It was officially listed in the National Register of Historic Places in 1972. In 2016, a nonprofit

The Denkmann-Hauberg House, also known as the Hauberg Estate, is located at 1300 Twenty-Fourth Street, Rock Island, Illinois. It is a twenty-thousand-square-foot mansion surrounded by ten acres. *Photo by Bruce Walters.*

organization, the Friends of Hauberg Civic Center Foundation, was created to oversee the preservation and sustainability of the Hauberg Estate, including the mansion and gardens.

John was a prolific public speaker. He gave more than three hundred speeches in his lifetime, the transcripts of which amount to more than 125 linear feet of paper. "And there are over 100,000 photographs and glass slides—it is amazing. Their life is very well documented," said Ms. Deb Kuntzi, director of the nonprofit organization Friends of Hauberg Civic Center Foundation (FOHCCF).

Susanne was extremely accomplished as well. She established the West End Settlement, the Rock Island YWCA and YMCA and children's camps (Camp Hauberg for the boys and Camp Archie Allen for the girls in Port Byron). In addition, she, along with her siblings, donated the funds to build the Denkmann Memorial Library at Augustana College.

"The house was originally going to be for Susanne Denkmann, two school teachers and a principal. Then she met John [Hauberg]. She was the lumber heiress; he was an attorney. They met at Bethany's Homes in Moline; they were on the same board. He proposed to her over the terrace gardens.

They both loved the outdoors. Soon after, they were married, went on their honeymoon, came back and moved in," said Kuntzi.

Susanne suffered from epilepsy and employed a nurse, known as Miss Ross, to help her. The family also employed a nanny, a Miss Vogt, for the children. "We've had paranormal groups and tours here; we had mediums here during our murder mysteries. They all concluded that there were two women and two men in the house. We know who the two women are: Miss Ross and Miss Vogt. We don't know who the two men were. When we were fighting to establish the Friends of Hauberg, I felt John and John Jr. around me all the time," Kuntzi said.

"The paranormal groups say that John is here," added Kuntzi. "He probably is. I hear footsteps upstairs [in her office on the third floor, which was his law office]."

According to Kuntzi, John isn't the only one who made his presence known. "It was interesting when we had the medium here. The event was over, it was around midnight. We asked him if he wanted to go to the carriage house. We were walking on the sidewalk. We get to the doors to the place, and he goes, 'Oh,' and I said, 'What?' And he said, 'There is a guy right in front of my face.' And I said, 'Is it Andrew?' And he said, 'Yes. He's telling me, I have to ask, before I can come in.' I say, 'That makes sense.'"

Dining room in the Hauberg Estate. *Photo by Bruce Walters.*

Andrew was the chauffeur, although he preferred to be called a driver. He also helped with the landscaping. Susanne brought him over from her parents' house, and he lived in the second-floor apartment at the carriage house.

"The carriage house was his whole space—he was very protective of it," Kuntzi said. "We do hear him over there. One time we turned off all the water at the place, and yet the pipes were still rattling. When the paranormal groups were there, they heard doorbells—there were no doorbells."

Surprised by the alleged spirit behavior, Kuntzi couldn't help but wonder why he was acting this way. "I asked the medium, 'Why is he scaring people?' and he said, 'Because they didn't ask permission to come in.' I then tell Andrew, 'You can't go scaring people anymore!'" She added, "I believe Andrew is the most interesting and the most active spirit around Hauberg."

Ariel Renee Young did about half a dozen investigations of the Hauberg Estates. One of the more unusual experiences she had was by a small bridge next to five small ponds in the wooded area by the house. Coincidentally, this wasn't far from where John Hauberg proposed to Susanne Denkmann.

As they began their investigation, the group began to see some unusual lights. "A bunch of people were seeing orbs all over the place. It was like having a starry night front in you," Young said.

Deb Kuntzi and the Friends of Hauberg Civic Center Foundation continue to preserve not only the Hauberg Estate but also the memory of John, Susanne, their family and their employees. "I believe they are here. I've been told they like what we are doing, but we do too many things at once. I've been told that when I have stress, Susanne helps me out," she said.

The Mysterious Fisherman of Credit Island

The Mississippi River is home to many islands, each with its own story. In the case of Credit Island, there are many. With so much life and activity that has taken place there, it's little surprise that, perhaps, something supernatural might linger throughout this 420-acre park in Southwest Davenport at 2301 West River Drive.

According to legend, Credit Island received its name in the 1700s when British and French traders brought their goods south from what is now modern-day Wisconsin. This included everything from firearms to footwear. The story goes that entire families came out to the island and made an exciting day of first shopping and then spending time with friends and family while enjoying the items that they had just purchased.

Of course, the Sauk and Meskwaki tribes who came there didn't pay in money. Rather, they traded for the goods by giving the traders furs procured from the lands that they roamed and hunted. Every year, goods were bought on credit, and the natives promised the traders that they would reward them well the next time. Sure enough, the traders' trust was rewarded when the natives came back with a stack of valuable furs at the next gathering. Over time, the island where the transactions always took place became known as Credit Island.

These good days weren't to last. By the early nineteenth century, American relations with the Sauks and Meskwakis were not always the best. In 1812, a combined British and Sauk force successfully attacked and repelled American forces coming upriver from St. Louis at Credit Island in an event that, appropriately enough, became known as the Battle of Credit Island.

Credit Island is located around 2200 West River Drive in Davenport, Iowa, and is 1.3 miles long. *Photo by Michael McCarty.*

Credit Island derived its name from the use of the island as an early Native America trading post. *Photo by Michael McCarty.*

In the 1830s, after the Sauks and Meskwakis were removed from the region, some of the white settlers from the east cleared land on Credit Island, tilled the land and tried their best to make farms there. Their endeavors were met with limited success, and by 1864, a man named John Offerman had purchased the island, turning it into a private park. He called it, appropriately enough, Offerman's Island, and it became a popular stop for steamboats and their passengers.

Ownership of the island changed hands a few more times over the next few decades, but it remained a popular spot for locals to gather. In 1903, a company called the Grand Island Park Company bought the island and built an amusement park there. This included tennis courts, a bowling alley and even a roller coaster. The following year, streetcar service was run there, allowing people to ride out to the island from a streetcar stop closer to their homes.

At some point during this time, a man named Jonas Walsh and his young son decided to go fishing on the island on a warm January day. The two really enjoyed ice fishing, and the area around Credit Island was a perfect place for them to go. The weather that day reminded them of spring days that would be coming soon. As they set out that morning, they both felt very fortunate to be able to take advantage of such a fine day.

Jonas was a friendly man who enjoyed a good conversation, especially about fishing. He and his son weren't the only ones out on the ice around the island, and Jonas made sure to spend some time visiting with the other people there.

As they sat at their fishing hole, Jonas noticed another fisherman nearby that he hadn't ever seen before. The man was sitting on a bucket; a hood attached to the heavy coat he was wearing obscuring his features. He seemed to be a little overdressed to Jonas, but it was still January and some people felt the cold a little more than others.

Walking over with his son, Jonas greeted the man. The fisherman didn't respond, seemingly focused on the hole in the ice in front of him.

"Have you caught anything?" Jonas asked.

"Nothing," the man replied.

"Huh. That's a shame. Plenty of daylight left, though, and I'm sure you'll get something yet." Jonas said, smiling. He glanced over at his son, who was trying his best to look down into the hole that the man was fishing out of. Seeing the line in the water made Jonas think of something.

"Say, what are you using for bait, mister?" he asked.

Illustration by Jason McLean.

"Nothing." The same reply as before. Jonas was a little taken aback. He knew that some people didn't like to share what they used for bait, just like some didn't like to talk about the best fishing spots. Still, there was a nicer way to do it than just ignore him and give him a non-answer.

The more Jonas thought about it, the more irritated he became. This guy was a real prize. The fisherman hadn't even looked up at him even once. What kind of a guy gives answers like that and doesn't even look you in the face?

"You know, pal…" Jonas's voice trailed off as he felt something grip his arm. Looking down, he saw it was his son. The boy's face was paler than the snow on the ground. "What's wrong, son?" he asked. His boy didn't get scared like that. What the hell could have done that to him? The boy just shook his head and pointed at the fisherman, his eyes wide.

Jonas looked hard at the man in the heavy coat. Suddenly, everything felt wrong somehow. He felt his legs begin to move before he had given it any thought. He began to circle around in front of the man, his eyes never leaving the stranger's hood. As he walked, Jonas was able to see inside the hood better. He kept waiting to see his face, but it always seems to be just out of sight.

Jonas was standing almost directly in front of the fisherman before he realized what the problem was: the hood was empty. Jonas just stared. There was no head, no face—no anything. Suddenly, the man's reply of "nothing" made so much more sense. A second later, the coat that was obviously empty, and yet also had clearly held *something*, fell to the ground, empty. The shirt, pants and boots collapsed next.

Oddly, he didn't feel afraid. Jonas walked over and stepped on the clothes, stomping on them with his boot. Jonas hoped that he would find something inside, but he knew that he wouldn't. Reaching down, he held up the coat that, until a few moments before, Jonas had sworn held a man. Now it was empty and seemingly had been all along.

What was it that Jonas Walsh saw that day? Was it the spirit of a long-ago trader who still enjoyed being on the island? Or was it just an old fisherman who had always fished on Credit Island and was determined to keep doing so long after their death? Like Jonas Walsh, we'll probably never know. For now, the truth behind the vanishing fisherman on Credit Island belongs to the island alone.

The Tinsmith Ghost
of Rock Island

There's nothing quite like moving into a new house. In most cases, a new buyer obviously likes it, otherwise they never would have bought it. They like the layout and the features. In an older home, people often talk about liking the character of the home. There's something about how it feels.

Still, it takes a little bit to get used to a new house. The first few weeks living there are like the first few dates with a longtime significant other. There's a mutual attraction and a willingness to move forward, but still a hesitancy. Personalities are being sounded out, and potential obstacles to the success of the relationship are managed. The rough edges still have to be sanded off.

Houses are much the same way. Furnaces kick on, air conditioners start up, floors creek, windows rattle, cupboard doors stick and more. These are all common things, but in a new environment, they can sound completely alien. After a little while, the new homeowner gets used to it and settles in comfortably. The unknown becomes the known.

But what happens when things occur that can't be explained? In 1887, Rock Island, Illinois, was a bustling, successful city. It was full of a thriving population with stable businesses. Life was good and people were happy. Albert Ames was one of them.

Albert Ames and his wife had just moved into a two-story house at 1428 Fourth Avenue. Albert was out of town for business a good deal of the time, so Mrs. Ames would be left to her own devices much of the time. Like many people, she probably spent the first few weeks unpacking and arranging her

Illustration by Jason McLean.

new home just so. Slowly, the house was becoming a comfortable new home. Gradually, she began becoming accustomed to the noises her new home made as it settled and creaked.

Then, one day, she heard footsteps. It was late at night, and something must have woken her up. She stirred, probably still a little disoriented from having just awoken. Suddenly, her body tensed as she heard it. Someone was moving through the house! She held her breath, listening. There it was again! She was sure that she hadn't imagined it that time. There was a soft, scraping sound, as if someone were trying to move stealthily through the house. Still, it couldn't have been anything serious. It was probably the wind or a tree branch scraping against the outside. Having made peace with yet another new noise, Mrs. Ames rolled over and went back to sleep.

The next night, Mrs. Ames was once again awoken in the night by what sounded like soft footsteps walking across the floor on the balls of their feet. Occasionally, there would come a loud crash from elsewhere in the house, like someone was tearing down walls. Once again, she told herself that the noises were nothing out of the ordinary—just the wind banging a shutter against the side of the house. It made sense. There was a rational explanation. Sure, they startled her, but any loud noise in a quiet room can do that. For her, it was just a new noise to get used to.

But they kept happening, and in spite of making perfectly good sense, Mrs. Ames couldn't find anything that could have made those noises. Even her idea of a slamming shutter stopped making sense when she noticed that it still happened when there was no wind blowing.

Slowly, the explanations that she gave herself were starting to make less and less sense. It was getting harder for her to apply rational explanations to these things. Then, as Mrs. Ames walked through the house one night, she was shocked to see a man standing in one of the bedrooms. Several feelings must have swept through her as the adrenaline started to course through her body. Mrs. Ames had an intruder in her home, and she was very, very alone.

Ames immediately demanded to know who the person was. The man simply stood there, saying nothing. It was as if someone had placed a statue wearing a man's clothes in the middle of one of her bedrooms. She tried talking to him again, no doubt asking questions and demanding that he leave her house. In an instant, he was gone. Disappeared. The stranger hadn't moved or tried to walk out past her. He was just…gone. It was as if he had just vanished like smoke in the wind.

After that, Mrs. Ames began to hear the noises more often. Much more disturbingly, she also began to see the mysterious man more frequently.

Although he was seen in different areas of the house, he would appear most often in the bedroom where she had first laid eyes on him.

Finally, it was too much to keep to herself. Mrs. Ames started to talk to a neighbor about her problem. She told them about the noises and described the man in the house. Mrs. Ames also made sure to tell them what he had been doing there, including the disappearing act and that he was showing up in that same bedroom all the time.

The neighbor listened politely to her story. They took a deep breath and exhaled. The man, the neighbor explained, sounded exactly like the previous occupant of the house. His name was Joseph P. Stroehle, a tin worker and stove salesman.

Although a relatively young man, he had become very ill. In spite of that, Joseph stubbornly kept working. His condition worsened, and on a return visit to the doctor, Joseph was informed that his illness was terminal. The young tin worker still refused to believe his diagnosis and pushed on. His will seemed to keep him going after that. Joseph was determined to keep going, and he continually drove himself on. However, sheer will can only carry a person so far. Eventually, the body will shut down in spite of whatever motivations the mind screams at it. In April 1886, Stroehle died, and he was buried at Chippiannock Cemetery just a few miles away.

Meeting Mrs. Ames's gaze, the neighbor told her that the bedroom where she kept seeing him was the one in which Stroehle had died. Mrs. Ames had been seeing a dead man in her house.

Two things in this world that people love are a good ghost story and gossip. News of the ghost spread quickly through the neighborhood and then made its way outward from there into the surrounding city. Neighbors who sat in the home with Mrs. Ames never saw the spirit themselves, but that's not to say that they didn't have experiences of their own. Several people who walked through the home claimed to have heard the creeping footsteps and loud crashes that Mrs. Ames had heard.

One man who went through the house had a particularly unnerving experience. He claimed that he was walking through the house by himself. After the man stepped from an empty room into an adjoining one, he closed the door behind himself. As soon as did, someone started knocking from the other side. He immediately grabbed the knob, turned and threw the door open. There was nothing there. The man stepped through, looking for someone who might have hidden somewhere close after knocking. Finding no one, the man was left to wonder who—or what—had been knocking on the door.

The haunted house became quite the attraction, and several local people came to watch the house from the outside, clogging the street. One night, it was estimated that there were about five hundred people watching the house, apparently just wanting to see the haunted house and maybe even catch a glimpse of something supernatural.

Mrs. Ames continued to hear the noises and see Joseph Stroehle. One night, while speaking with some house guests, she suddenly let out a loud scream. She said that she had seen the ghost again, but no one else present did.

Finally, enough was enough. At least for a few nights, Mrs. Ames would not stay at her house. She also sent word to Albert, who was on business in Kansas City at that time, to come home. He did as fast as he could, and he must have been surprised to see the mass of people outside of his house.

After being informed of what was going on, he allowed seven young men to stay in the house as a group, possibly in the hope that they would discover something that would explain the entire situation. In spite of hoping for the best, the ghost never appeared.

Soon, the excitement over the haunted house on Fourth Avenue died down. There were other things to do and better ways to occupy people's time. While there were almost definitely some people who believed in the whole story, others took a more skeptical approach. Not only did they not believe that the house was haunted, but they also proposed that either Mrs. Ames was hallucinating or she was making the whole thing up. The jury is still out.

Albert Ames and his wife disappeared quietly into the mists of time, fading out of our knowledge. Was Mrs. Ames lonely and seeking attention? Did she make the entire story up for her own entertainment? Or did she really see the ghost of her home's former owner?

Existing evidence shows that Stroehle lived there, as well as shows what he did for a living. As far as his spirit haunting his former home, the answers to those questions are open to interpretation. The house has long since been torn down. But does that necessarily mean that Joseph Stroehle's restless soul went with it?

If any of you are curious, you could always go and find out. Perhaps, if you stand on the old corner in the wee hours of the morning, you'll hear the soft shuffle of feet across concrete and see the shadow of a tinsmith who still walks the same places he did more than one hundred years ago.

Alice French House

The Quad Cities has produced several well-known individuals who made their mark on the world. In the late nineteenth and early twentieth centuries, it would have been hard to find a more well-known name than Alice Virginia French.

"Alice Virginia French was considered to be one of the foremost story writers of the world at that time. Alice French, who wrote under the pseudonym 'Octave Thanet,' was an eminent writer who had twenty books published. She often wrote about life in Davenport as the fictional town of Fairport and the author of *Stories of a Western Town*, which is considered to be her best work," said Doug Smith, author of the book *Davenport* said.

Alice's father, George Henry French, had a successful leather business in Boston. In 1856, he moved his family to Davenport at 321 East Tenth Street, where it didn't take him long to rebuild his former success. His business ventures earned him an excellent living. His lumber company even received the contract to build Camp McClellan, the first Civil War training camp in Davenport. French was also the founder of the Eagle Plow Manufacturing Company, a very successful manufacturing facility during that era of Quad City history.

Politically, French did just as well. He was elected treasurer of the Davenport school board twelve times and served two terms as mayor of Davenport during the Civil War. In addition, he was also a president of the First National Bank and the Davenport and St. Paul Railroad.

The Alice French House, located at 321 East Tenth Street in Davenport, Iowa. Alice French wrote a book of photography, nine collections of short stories and seven full-length novels. She often wrote about Davenport, Iowa, as the fictional town of Fairport. *Photo by Michael McCarty.*

George had set an amazing example for his children to follow, and Alice was more than up to the challenge. Her first published writing was a short story, "Hugo's Waiting," printed in the *Davenport Gazette* on February 18, 1871, under the pen name Frances Essex. That was only the beginning of a long and illustrious literary career.

French would eventually write a book of photography, nine collections of short stories and seven full-length novels. Her work regularly appeared in the leading publications of the day, with several of her short stories and essays appearing in *Scribner's Monthly*, *Lippinicott's Monthly*, *Sunday Afternoon*, *Atlantic Monthly* and *Harper's Bazaar*.

Her social circle was made up of the upper crust of not only local Quad City society but also national society. She counted both Andrew Carnegie and President Theodore Roosevelt among her close personal friends. When she got older, she focused her efforts primarily on social work, and she wasn't afraid to ask her prestigious friends for support now and then. Said Doug Smith:

In January of 1900, Alice French wrote to a personal friend, Andrew Carnegie, seeking a small donation for the library. This led to the construction of our first free public library at Main and Fourth streets in 1903.

Once among the most famous, respected and well-to-do of ladies of the Midwest, it was Alice French who, on November 4, 1910, hosted a breakfast in her home for former President of the United States, Theodore Roosevelt before he gave a speech in Central Park before a crowd of about 6,000.

Alice French was also with the Davenport Group, an organization of writers in the early part of the twentieth century. Said J. Douglas Miller, local filmmaker and historian:

Arthur Davidson Ficke, Susan Glaspell, Floyd Dell and George Cram Cook were members. Cook and Glaspell discovered and produced the first plays of Eugene O'Neill in Provincetown and New York. Cook and Glaspell also were the discoverers of one of the first great feminist writers of the 20th Century, Edna St. Vincent Millay. Cook was arrested once in Davenport for swimming nude in the Dillon Fountain while visiting his Davenport Friends. Their dream was to come back to Davenport and create a "New Athens."

Although she spent part of her time in Arkansas, Alice always considered Davenport to be her true home. Despite her wealth and success, her home here was relatively plain when compared to others. Located in what is now downtown Davenport, Alice's house was a modest home built in a combination of the Queen Anne and Colonial Revival styles. Regardless, Alice loved it, and it served her needs well.

In later life, she developed diabetes, and complications from the disease led to the loss of one leg and most of her eyesight. She died on January 9, 1934, and was buried in the French family plot at Oakdale Memorial Gardens.

Some say that not all members of the French family are lying quietly in their graves. It is rumored that the spirit of George Henry French lingers in Alice's former home, a house that he once owned.

Some people have claimed to have seen a distinguished-looking gentleman dressed in an old-fashioned suit standing in the parlor, while others have seen lights mysteriously turning on and off. Allegedly, doors slam shut by themselves throughout the house as well. Visitors going into the basement have felt cold spots in an otherwise warm space. Perhaps most terrifying, people in the home have heard mysterious and otherworldly voices.

Do members of the French family still walk the corridors and rooms of the home? Are they still engaging in deep conversation with one another, long after their deaths?

The Alice French house is a private residence and not open to the public. Perhaps, in the quiet of the night, the owners might be able to listen hard against the silence and find out for themselves.

Renwick Mansion

For the happy couple, it was finally the big day at the Renwick Mansion, located at 901 Tremont Avenue in Davenport, and the place had seldom looked finer. The summer heat did nothing to dampen the spirits of the guests that day.

Regardless, the groom's grandmother felt as if she were in a dream. Her gaze caressed every surface as she stood, remembering a much different time in the life of the nine-thousand-square-foot and more than 140-year-old mansion. She had been much younger back then, and the Italianate Revival–style building was a mental health and nursing facility. She later told the current owners, Dane and Sarah Moulton, that patients had been housed on the second floor. Sometimes they would say that when everyone was in their rooms and silence fell like a curtain over the building, the patients would hear someone walking the halls despite the fact that no one was out of their rooms and no staff members were present.

The Moultons had heard stories that the house was haunted before they bought it in 2017. They didn't mind. They had fallen in love with the building and were more than happy to purchase a property rich in history and charm.

Originally built in 1877 by local lumber baron and businessman William Renwick, the house boasts eight bedrooms, a three-story grand staircase and a tower room on the fourth floor that showcases a stunning view of downtown Davenport and the Mississippi River.

In 1900, the Renwick family moved out, and the home became part of the all-girls St. Katherine's School campus directly next door. After the school relocated to Bettendorf, the former mansion and school campus were turned into a mental health and nursing facility. In the early 2000s, the property was renovated to its former glory, later being purchased by Iowa senator Joseph Seng in 2007. Seng opened the property for public rental, available for weddings, reunions and overnight stays.

After Senator Seng's untimely death in 2016, the mansion was put up for sale again and bought by the Moultons the following year. Ever since, they have continued to use the Renwick as a venue for weddings, concerts and comedy shows.

The Moultons had seen footage of paranormal investigations carried out at the mansion but were made keenly aware of the Renwick's haunted reputation by a close family member. "Sarah's mother was remarried at the

The Renwick Mansion, circa 1890. At its completion, the Renwick residence featured two stories rising above a high basement and surmounted by a seventy-foot tower, an ornamented roundabout with a carriage porch, piazzas, balconies and lookouts adorned with beautiful cornice work and cresting. *From* Davenport Iowa History *(Doug Smith).*

Renwick before we purchased it," recalled Dane Moulton. "Her sister stayed on the third floor and said that she woke up and there was an old man and woman standing in the corner of the room."

Over the past few years, the Moultons have hosted several paranormal investigations of their own at the Renwick. Many of these groups have captured disembodied voices on their audio recording equipment. The members of one group, Ghost Crier, were asking the ghosts questions in a second-floor bedroom. When they reviewed the recordings later, they could hear someone distinctly saying, "Sarah's house."

Cassie Steffen, founding member of the Broadway Paranormal Society, had a particularly memorable experience using what investigators call a GeoBox. According to Steffen, "[The GeoBox]…generates…radio waves, and the spirits can talk through it, but in really clear, booming voices usually."

Hearing a GeoBox being used upstairs, Steffen decided to go and join the session. As they asked the spirits questions, they waited expectantly for any answers that any prospective ghosts might decide to give through the device. After a few moments, the box very clearly and loudly said, "Cassie."

One of the members there asked if the spirit speaking had something to say to Steffen. According to Steffen herself, "The GeoBox said, real loud, 'Get out!'" She didn't have to be told twice and promptly left.

According to another paranormal investigator, Nick Simon, also with the Broadway Paranormal Society, he had experiences in the mansion's basement. "If you go all the way to the east side of the basement, there is an old coal room in the back. If you stand in the coal room and look out, you can see shadows dart across the room every once in a while."

Several paranormal groups that have investigated the Renwick said that they encountered the shade or shape of a small girl. Some visitors have also claimed to have seen her. On one occasion, the Moultons were renting the mansion for a baby shower. "There was once, after a baby shower when our clients were cleaning up…a little girl asked her mom who 'the little girl is,' but there was no other little girl," Sarah said.

While the Moultons say they haven't had anything happen to them in the basement, they did say that the daughter of a previous owner did. She said that on several occasions, she went down there and found that the covering of a particular light fixture had been removed. Somehow, it had been placed on the other side of the room.

Comedian Chris Schlichting has booked and hosted the comedy show *Tomfoolery on Tremont* monthly at the Renwick Mansion since 2018. Several of the comedians have claimed to have experienced supernatural activity, including Mike Brody.

"While [Brody] was on stage performing, a water bottle cap appeared to be pushed off the stool on stage," Schlichting said. "The cap was in the center of the stool and had been there for over half the show. It was so noticeable that Mike stopped his performance and asked if anyone else saw that." The Moultons confirmed the story, explaining that an audience member that night had even recorded the entire incident on Snapchat. This wouldn't be the last time a strange incident occurred during a performance.

"On a different show, while the comic was on stage, the shutters on the windows behind the comic were shut," Schlichting related. "At one point during the show, the wooden blinds on the shudders opened and then closed. Multiple audience members brought it up after the show."

Dane and Sarah, who were bartending in the back of the room at the time, heard the reports from audience members almost right after this had happened. According to them, "As skeptics we explained there was a vent

The Renwick Mansion, located at 901 Tremont Avenue, looms on the bluff in Davenport, Iowa. The four-story Italianate Revival–style house was originally built in 1877 by local lumber baron and businessman William Renwick. *Photo by Michael McCarty.*

below the stage that probably forced the air to do that; however, we're not sure if that would be possible after testing it."

According to another story, a former housekeeper lived on the third floor of the mansion. On several occasions, she claimed to hear the steps creaking behind her as she went up to her rooms, almost as if there was someone following right behind. When the housekeeper turned around to confront who it was, there was no one there.

While open-minded to the supernatural, the Moultons prefer to find logical explanations to any phenomena experienced in the house. "The floorboards are creaky, and Dane thinks that when they are stepped on, they have some flex to them where they stay down for a second after and pop up a second later," Sarah said.

The Renwick Mansion stands as a mute testimony to the splendor and style of a bygone era. From its lofty perch atop the river bluffs, it has seen the city grow and expand around it, watching as history unfolded in the Mississippi River Valley below. While some of that same history has been wiped away and forgotten outside its limestone walls, a part of the past may still walk through the well-kept mansion halls within.

The Haunted History
of Phi Kappa Chi

College fraternities have the reputation of being *Animal House*-type places where students ride motorcycles up stairwells and have obnoxiously loud parties wearing togas and drinking plenty of spirits.

Phi Kappa Chi, however, is a fraternity of professional men who want to become doctors in their chosen field of chiropractic. They're dedicating their lives to the pursuit of helping people get better and are very, very serious about doing so.

These young men are building reputations of respect and trust with both the community they live in and the wider world. They are quite possibly the very last people that you would ever expect to say that they live in what may have been one of the most haunted houses in the Quad Cities—or least it *was*, but we will get back to that later.

Phi Kappa Chi is a chiropractic fraternity associated closely with Palmer College of Chiropractic in Davenport, Iowa. Palmer is a notoriously difficult school to get through, and to do so demands the absolute dedication of its students.

In 1969, the fraternity bought a relatively modest home at 723 Main Street to become a residence for some of its members. They were probably excited to get it. It was big enough to hold several members and was located within easy walking distance of the Palmer campus, where the fraternity brothers worked and studied.

After the sale was finalized, the first eager members moved in and made themselves at home. Almost immediately, inexplicable events began to take

The Phi Kappa Chi fraternity house was located at 723 Main Street, Davenport, Iowa. The two-story residence was a fraternity house at Palmer College of Chiropractic from 1969 to 2020. *Photo by Michael McCarty.*

place. One day, Vernon Gielow, who was the public relations director for Palmer in the early 1970s, was in the basement of the frat house. He was going about his business when he distinctly heard the sound of the front door opening upstairs, followed by footsteps walking across the floor.

Thinking that it was the paperboy or maybe some other visitor, he quickly went upstairs to greet them. When he got to the front door, however, he found it was firmly closed, and there was no one else around. Who—or what—had made those sounds?

The stories of supernatural phenomena happening in the house had been quietly circulating around the fraternity brothers for years at that point. But these were professional men. None of them wanted to be ridiculed or thought to be delusional. They had reputations and professional images to maintain. And yet several of them had undeniably experienced something in that house.

One of the fraternity brothers, a young man from South Africa, claimed that he always heard noises all over the house, like someone was always moving around. He clearly heard footsteps moving through the house and doors opening and closing. Living in a house with other people, the young student expected that. However, he probably didn't expect to hear it when he was there by himself.

Once, while sitting another student, they heard the fraternity office door open. Soon after, they heard the sounds of papers shuffling and someone moving around. Curious, the two men got up to see who it was. When they arrived at the office door, the two students discovered that it was closed and securely locked.

Several of the other resident fraternity brothers also claimed to have experienced this same phenomenon. Doors opened and closed without anyone near them, and disembodied footsteps would move throughout the house, with no visible sign of what was making them. Others, like Vernon Gielow, said they heard the sound of the kitchen cupboards opening and closing.

Another time, a fraternity member was sitting in his attic room when he heard footsteps climb the stairs to the bathroom. The door opened and closed, and then the footsteps left again and went back downstairs.

Soon after, another student knocked on his door and entered. The attic resident asked his fellow student who else was in the house. Puzzled, the student replied that they were the only ones there. What, then, had been walking through the house?

Perhaps even more disturbing was the fact that the unseen footsteps seemed to be being made by at least two separate people. Some claimed that the footsteps they heard were light and carefree, while others said that they heard heavy, angry steps that were more like stomps.

Footsteps were far from the only phenomenon that manifested itself at the frat house. One night, two students were in the living room talking when a set of glass doors that led out onto a second-story balcony opened by themselves. Naturally, they thought that it was just the wind. Continuing their conversation, one of them got up and closed them again. Making sure that they were securely shut, he sat back down.

A few minutes later, the doors swung open again. Puzzled, the students closed the doors again and this time pushed a heavy chiropractic adjustment table in front of them. Satisfied that a casual gust of wind wouldn't blow the doors open again, they resumed their conversation. A short while later, however, they heard the doors *click*. Turning to look, they watched with a mixture of amazement and horror as the doors slowly opened, pushing the adjustment table across the floor as they did.

Many of the brothers felt like they were being watched, both inside the house or just outside it. For some of them, they also experienced deep feelings of dread around the house.

Perhaps, in at least a few cases, they were right to be afraid. One night, a student was in bed studying when he heard footsteps downstairs. He quietly listened as they made their way steadily up the stairs. The young man had heard footsteps on the stairs several times before, but there was something *off* about these. He began to tense as they grew closer. When they stopped outside of his bedroom door, he began to feel the first tingles of fear.

The student held his breath, listening hard. His eyes widened when he heard the door open. However, the student clearly saw that the door was still physically closed. How could that be? As he stared at the door, the footsteps started again. The young man could feel his heart pounding in his chest as he heard *something* cross the room toward him. Like the door, he clearly heard the footsteps, but there was absolutely nothing there. The unseen thing stopped right in front of the bed.

Terrified, the man didn't know what to do. He could feel a kind of presence there, like someone was standing there, glaring down at him. Despite his fear, the man didn't want to admit that there was something there that he couldn't see—or even that this was happening.

So, slowly and cautiously, he turned over and faced away. After what seemed like an eternity, the feeling finally eased. That little bit of relief was all it took to motivate the student to get up and find one of his fraternity brothers. It felt so much better being with another living, breathing human being. Regardless, the experience left him shaken and uneasy.

Another resident of the home claimed that he had gone to bed after a party at the fraternity. Some time later, he woke up in the early hours of the morning. The resident remembered that he had felt very cold. As he tried to wake himself up a little, the man suddenly felt something physically grab him by the throat. His adrenaline surged as the unseen assailant started to squeeze harder, choking him. He tried desperately to call for help but couldn't make a sound.

Then, just as suddenly as it had begun, the student felt the invisible hand release his throat. As he sat there, gulping in air, he heard the front door slam, almost as if his unseen attacker had left. Quickly, he got out of bed and began to search every corner of the house. Everyone else in the house that night was fast asleep. There was no one else there.

Deeply disturbed by his experience, the young man went downstairs, turned on all the lights and stayed up until morning. Later, when he began to tell his fraternity brothers about his experience that night, he learned that others had experienced the same thing.

Although they didn't want to admit it, the fraternity brothers had no explanation for the things going on within their house. It defied all explanations that they could put forward, except for one. Reluctantly, they had little choice but to conclude that their house was haunted.

Still, if there was something supernatural at the frat house, then why was it there? There had to be an explanation. To find one, they began to research the history of the home. They spent hours combing through the abstract for the home and exhaustively researched city directories and courthouse records.

Like so much land in the area, the ground that house sat on originally belonged to Antoine LeClaire, one of the founding fathers of the city of Davenport. Later, it was owned by the original St. Luke's Hospital, which stood nearby.

After the home was built, it was occupied for years by Dr. William A. Stoecks, a prominent doctor in Davenport for many years. Stoecks ran a successful practice and served on the medical boards for both St. Luke's Hospital and the Scott County Medical Society. He also served several terms as city physician, an elected position that put him in charge of the city's overall medical well-being. Later in life, he became wheelchair-bound, and buzzers were installed throughout the house so he could call for assistance no matter where he was. He lived there until his death in 1961.

Later owners included a railroad clerk and his wife. The clerk allegedly abused her, and she eventually divorced him. She continued to live in the house until 1968. Was one of these former residents behind the phenomena at 723 Main Street? Or was it someone else?

In 2019, authors Michael McCary and Mark McLaughlin reported in their book, *Ghosts of the Quad Cities*, that some people claim that the frat house was haunted by the ghost of a homeless man, brought inside due to freezing temperatures in the 1930s, back when it was a private residence.

"There was a guy in the house who died during the winter. Unexplained snow tracks inside the house have been reported," said Kyle Dickson, the former assistant director of the German American Heritage Center.

The fame that the house's haunted reputation brought it eventually traveled outside the Quad Cities. In May 1972, occult writer Irene Hughes, a well-known Chicago medium, came to investigate the house.

As educated as the fraternity brothers had become about the history of their house, they did not specialize in the supernatural. They already knew that they were out of their depth and understood the value of having an expert take a look at the situation.

The remains of the Phi Kappa Chi house after being leveled. *Photo by Michael McCarty.*

Accompanied by author Brad Steiger, Hughes was taken to the frat house without being given any information about the background of the home or the people living there. When they arrived, Hughes began to walk slowly from room to room. As she did, she began to tell the assembled fraternity brothers about the history of their home with uncanny accuracy. Soon enough, they began to tell them even more.

Hughes said that although she felt that there was more than one spirit at the home, the strongest one was a medical doctor. She said that the spirit told her that he didn't believe in chiropractic and greatly frowned on its practice. He also told Hughes that he felt the young men were disturbing him in his home.

That a medical doctor from the early part of the twentieth century disagreed with the practice of chiropractic medicine probably came as no great surprise to the fraternity. Many medical professionals of that era openly spoke against it, some more harshly than others.

Irene Hughes wasn't the only celebrity to take an interest in the house. The Amazing Kreskin, a world-famous mentalist, also investigated the frat house. In 1991, Michael McCarty, one of the coauthors of this book, visited the Phi Kappa Chi house as part of a project with Kreskin.

"I first met The Amazing Kreskin when I worked at the Funny Bone Comedy Club in Davenport, Iowa," McCarty said. "I was working as a promotion coordinator. I needed to help Kreskin to find a location for a séance he wanted to do for the media. I needed to find a Quad City haunted house for the event. So, I arranged for his séance to take place at the frat house, since I'd read so many articles by Jim Arpy about it."

Local television news crews, newspaper reporters and even some DJs all attended the séance. Kreskin asked the Phi Kappa Chi students to sit around a large table and then demonstrated the kind of activities that would occur during a séance. "The hair on the back of my neck stood up during the presentation," McCarty said. "I felt a sudden chill come over me. Something definitely felt unnatural about the place. I was against a far corner of the building, but I kept feeling like someone was behind me during the show, I even turned to look, but behind me was just the wall."

When Michael McCarty was working on *Ghosts of the Quad Cities*, he brought his digital Cannon to take a photo for the book. He went in the early afternoon and snapped a photo of the front of the house. "It wasn't very spooky," he recalled. "It looked like your typical two-story house from the Gold Coast District. I wanted something with a little more atmosphere. So I decided to go back at night and shoot the photo again. I climbed up the many steps, and the moonlight was shining through the trees. I took a photo. We actually ran both the night and day photos for the book. The weird thing is this: at the time I shot the night photo, I didn't see it, but a faint orb caught on film, appeared near the Tiki torch and window by the door."

On June 11, 2020, Phi Kappa Chi and the other houses on the block were demolished to make green space for Palmer College of Chiropractic. "The place was very special to me," McCarty said. "It was the inspiration for two of my books, *Ghosts of the Quad Cities* and *Conversations with Kreskin*. Seeing the frat leveled and only bricks remaining was very sad indeed. It was like losing an old friend."

Today, there is little to remind the casual observer of the house that once stood at 723 Main Street. There is less than that to suggest that something beyond the ordinary happened there. Did one of the former residents still haunt the home? Was it their footsteps heard walking around the house and their presences felt? Perhaps it was all of them, still so attached to their beloved home in death that they could not bear to leave.

With the house gone, we'll probably never know. However, like the spirits that once walked there, the memory of the fraternity house still haunts us.

PART II

STRANGE CREATURES, STRANGE HAPPENINGS AND UFO SIGHTINGS

Curious Creatures

GIANT CATFISH

There are more than one hundred different species of fish in the stretch of the Mississippi River that winds its way through the Quad Cities region. Over time, both man-made forces and the forces of nature itself have changed the river. The fish have little choice but to change as well, adapting to their surroundings in order to survive.

Perhaps it is this constant pressure to adapt and thrive in their environment that has given rise to the numerous stories of giant catfish that have been caught in the muddy ol' river. While it sounds like some kind of a fish tale told by a couple of fishermen at a pub, there have been several reports in local newspapers and TV stations of peculiar catfish caught in the Quad Cities over the years.

According to an article by Jeremiah Haas, a reporter working for the *Rock Island Argus* and *Moline Dispatch*, there have been many documented catches of catfish that exceed sixty pounds. "There are reports from the 1800s of catfish in excess of 100 pounds being caught commonly," Haas added.

Said Doug Smith, author the book *Davenport* and webmaster for the "Davenport Iowa History" Facebook page: "In April of 1909, Frank and Clarence Healy of Muscatine, Iowa, came across a giant catfish lying near the shore in a slough a few miles below that city. Frank succeeded in getting his fingers in the gills of the fish, which promptly swam away with him. Clarence came to the rescue with a hatchet and the fish was stunned and landed. It weighed 40 pounds."

In April 1909, Frank and Clarence Healy of Muscatine, Iowa, came across a forty-pound catfish lying near the shore in a slough a few miles below that city. *From* Davenport Iowa History *(Doug Smith)*.

The stories are numerous. A Quad Cities man named Ron Lane once caught a big catfish weighing thirty-five pounds. In May 2016, Samuel Brown caught a forty-five -pound flathead catfish on the shore near Lock and Dam 15 at the Rock Island Arsenal after wrestling to catch the very big fish.

One year later, near the same spot on June 24, 2017, Brown caught another river monster just east of the roller dam. This time, the flathead catfish weighed nearly sixty pounds.

Donald Goering of Davenport boasts an even more impressive record. On June 29, 2018, he caught a fifty-five-pound, forty-five-inch flathead catfish on the Mississippi River near Credit Island. He weighed and measured it at the Credit Island Bait Shop and again on his home scales before eventually releasing it back into the river. In 2019, Mr. Goering caught a fifty-pound catfish. His wife, Samantha, took a photo with his cellphone and posted it on Facebook just before the cell ended up on the bottom of the muddy river near Credit Island. He also released that monster catfish back into the Mighty Mississippi.

Above: Donald Goering's fifty-five-pound, forty-five-inch flathead catfish caught near Credit Island, Davenport, Iowa, on June 29, 2018. *Courtesy of Donald Goering.*

Right: Donald Goering in 2019 with his fifty-pound catfish. His wife, Samantha, took this photo with his cellphone and posted it on Facebook moments before the cell ended up on the bottom Mississippi River. *Photo by Samantha Goering.*

Peter Robinson, aka "The Fish Guy," caught a giant catfish that he claimed weighed fifty pounds. He then proceeded to carry the big fish through downtown Davenport near the Skybridge. He commemorated the event by getting a tattoo on his forearm of himself riding a catfish with the date he caught it, "3-2-19," inked above it.

While local newspaper articles and news broadcasts gained him instant celebrity, local law enforcement branded him with instant infamy. When they discovered that he had noodled the giant catfish without a license (that is, caught the fish with his bare hands), they fined him $93.75.

PEPIE

Early Native Americans warned settlers of a large, serpent-like creature inhabiting the shadowy depths of midwestern lakes. The monster is called Pepie, after Lake Pepin, which forms the border between Minnesota and Wisconsin along the Mississippi River. Pepie, it is said, lives here.

For the past 150 years, the legend of Pepie has grown to epic proportions, even having a $50,000 reward being offered for the capture of the creature. The infamous monster has even been spotted in Muscatine, Iowa.

Authors Chad Lewis and Noah Voss wrote a book about the river monster called *Pepie: The Lake Monster of the Mississippi River*. Mr. Lewis, who has written numerous books about legends and supernatural occurrences in the Midwest, had much insight into the Pepie legend.

"Sightings of the mysterious Pepie beast tend to fall into two main categories," Lewis explained. "Most of those who are fortunate (or unfortunate) enough to catch a glimpse of the water monster describe the creature as having a long neck and head sticking straight out of the water. Its huge-humped body, which can range from 10 to 40 feet long, is almost always partially submerged. This type of sighting is similar to what people may think of as a Loch Ness Monster–type beast."

"The second type of sighting comes in the form of what seems like some sort of giant snake or eel-like creature," added Lewis. "Witnesses report that this snake shaped beast is between 20 and 40 feet long with a diameter of 12 to 24 inches….Many witnesses describe the color of Pepie as being a dark green, brown or black, allowing it to blend in with other native fish. It is unclear whether witnesses are simply viewing the creature from different angles and viewpoints, or perhaps they are spotting completely separate creatures."

Mr. Lewis continued:

> During the late 1800s and early 1900s, sightings of these aquatic beasts in the Mississippi River set off a firestorm of controversy; both experts and laypersons alike scrambled to come to grips with just exactly what witnesses were seeing.
>
> Skeptics tried to explain away all sightings as misidentifications, hoaxes or complete delusion on the part of the observer. At the same time, those who actually laid eyes on these beasts held firm in their belief that what they saw did not fit easily into any known classification. Thanks to the fantastical stories of the local newspapers, which warned of giant man-

Illustration by Jason McLean.

eating fish patrolling the Mississippi waters, protective parents forbade their children from playing near the river. Evidence of the killer fish was soon provided when several recovered bodies of drowning victims actually had what appeared to be claw and scratch marks around their ankles and calves. The belief was that these unsuspecting victims were out fishing or swimming in the river when the serpent latched on to their legs and dragged them out to their watery grave.

In June of 1886, the Anita Tribune *newspaper published a brief article about a weird sea serpent sighting near Muscatine. Two fishermen were enjoying a day at the river when they spotted a "river monster" dwelling in the water. Of course, the skeptical newspaper claimed that it must have been a "case of the snakes in its worst form."*

Amazingly, no further details were provided so the reader was left to imagine the size, shape, and coloration of this monster.

Thankfully the long-held fear and avoidance of the river has mostly subsided over the years, and today the Mississippi is a hopping place for fishing, hiking, boating, camping, and recreation. Many of the serpent legends and cautionary tales of the river have all been nearly forgotten—yet every time I am in the Mississippi River, I can't help but imagine that each piece of driftwood or rogue tree branch that brushes up against my legs are actually the long tentacles of some killer serpent just waiting to drag me to my death.

COUGAR SIGHTINGS

During the 1980s, a local newscaster reported that they saw a cougar in their backyard. Suddenly, reports of a big cat were pouring in from all over the Iowa and Illinois Quad Cities. Surely this had to be a case of mistaken identity? Maybe it was a trick of the light that made a large tomcat look bigger than it was, or maybe someone who was half-asleep had made a mistake. After all, cougars didn't live here, right?

Maybe not in the modern era, but according to local historian Doug Smith, the region played host to a surprising array of wildlife:

Back in the earliest descriptions of the area which is now Davenport, writers and newspaper editors penned numerous stories about bears, prairie chickens and even some kind of a beautiful parrot found here, but now extinct due to its obvious lack of camouflage.

Furthermore, it was not uncommon in frontier Iowa to find deer, elk, panther and lynx. Contrary to what is commonly espoused, bison or buffalo were not found in our area, nor east of Council Bluffs as they fed on the "buffalo grass" of the western great plains.

Other wild cats have been spotted in the area as well According to Wildcat Den State Park ranger Jordan Yaley, "Wildcat Den State Park got

Illustration by Jason McLean.

its name from pioneer settlers that lived and worked in this area in the late 1800s and early 1900s. The story is that local ranchers would drive cattle through this area along Pine Creek, and they would have to pass by an area known as 'Wildcat Den.' This area got that name as a result of wild cats that would be spotted by ranchers as they passed through."

There are actually three wildcats native to Iowa: the bobcat, the lynx and the mountain lion—the bobcat is the only one with an established population currently. Of course, that says nothing about anything that might just be passing through.

In 2011, a trail camera in the eastern portion of Clinton County, just northeast of the Quad Cities, caught a crystal-clear image of a mountain lion in the area. The Iowa Department of Natural Resources confirmed the footage, stating that the animal was more than likely on its way somewhere else and wouldn't stay to take up residence.

Up until that point, most Iowans, including several experienced outdoor enthusiasts, would have very confidently stated that no cougars lived within the borders of the state. Without the photographic evidence backing up the claim, the sighting would have probably just been simply laughed off.

But the animal sightings keep getting bigger and better over time. In addition to several more confirmed sightings of cougars, a large male black bear made its way through the region in 2020. Affectionately nicknamed Bruno, the bear spent several days in the region, gradually making its way south.

Animals refuse to accept the boundaries imposed on them by human expectation. Just because someone thinks that a bear should only live in the Wisconsin woods, or a cougar resides on a Colorado mountainside, does not mean that the animal will conform to their opinion. They simply move through the world, not recognizing a more rural housing development as a big cat no-go zone. For them, it is simply another section of the woods to explore as they strive to survive.

BIGFOOT

According to the folklore of many Native American tribes throughout the United States and Canada, the great North American wilderness is home to a giant creature. It walks on two legs and shows the intelligence of a man yet exhibits the enormous strength of an ape. As European settlers pushed west across the United States, they also began to have encounters with the strange, hairy being.

In the Quad City region, the oldest report was actually published in a Connecticut newspaper on September 27, 1869:

> *Considerable excitement exists in East Davenport and Gilbert Town [Bettendorf] in consequence of a wild boy, who has been seen by several veracious individuals, prowling about the woods at the back of Judge Grant's farm and on the river's bank and islands. About a week ago, a man returning from a shooting excursion saw what he at first took for some wild animal crouching by the bank of the river, it suddenly plunged in and emerged with a fish which it devoured ravenously. Getting closer to it he saw that it was a boy, apparently about 15 or 16, entirely without clothes, and covered with light sandy hair or silky appearance. He plainly saw the face, and describes it as revoltingly ugly and brutal in its aspect. He attempted to approach it, but the creature became alarmed, and taking to the water, swam to a neighboring island, and hid in the sedges. On returning home he gave information, and a close lookout has been kept. The creature, whatever it may be, has been seen twice.*

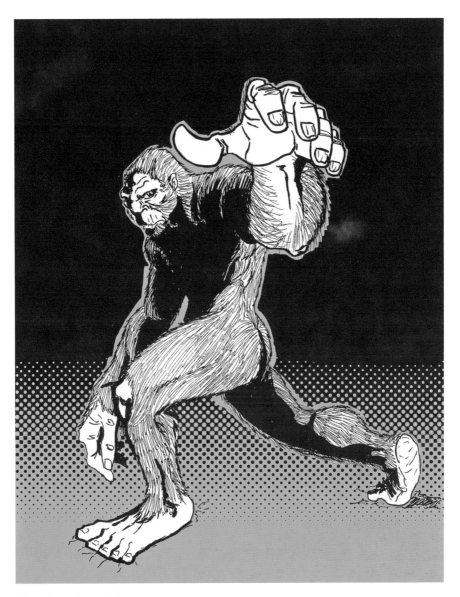

Illustration by Jason McLean.

In modern times, the first publicly reported case of the creature was in 1958, when Andrew Genzoli, a newspaper reporter in Northern California, wrote a series of articles about giant footprints found by construction workers in the region. They also reported a large, unknown creature throwing incredibly heavy objects with ease, including a 450-pound oil drum.

Molds were taken of the footprints, which measured seven inches wide by eighteen inches long. Based on this, the creature received the name by which it would become best known: Bigfoot. Over the next several decades, Bigfoot sightings continued to be reported throughout California, Seattle and Washington State. Many individuals began to associate the mountains and the vast acres of thick forest with the creature. Despite this, Bigfoot continued to be seen in areas all across the rest of the United States.

According to testimonials given to the Bigfoot Field Researchers Organization (BFRO), the creature has continued to visit the Quad Cities area. Since 1995, the goal of BFRO is to study the Bigfoot phenomenon by collecting as much information and empirical evidence about the creature as it possibly can. Toward that end, the organization has amassed an extensive collection of firsthand accounts with the creature, including some that stretch over a period of several decades in this region.

In 1969, a Bigfoot-like creature was seen in a rock quarry near Hampton, Illinois. In 1981, the creature was seen by a man delivering newspapers in Eldridge, Iowa. Perhaps one of the more compelling cases occurred in 1989, an experience that seems to defy logical explanation.

A camper, who will be referred to as Stan, was camping comfortably near the Wapsipinicon River with his girlfriend. He was an experienced woodsman and hunter who was more than comfortable in the wooded regions of northern Scott County. After a day enjoying the river, the couple decided to call it a day and crawled into their tent. As they had both the tent and the surrounding area to themselves, Stan and his girlfriend began to… well, do what young couples are known to do by themselves.

Suddenly, from out of nowhere came a deafening roar. It was loud and piercing and primal. It was a cry that should have been left in the Stone Age, uttered by a hungry predator prowling for humankind's ancestors.

The hair on Stan's neck stood on end. In all of his years in the outdoors, he had never heard anything that sounded like that. What was even worse was that it sounded so close, no more than a few dozen feet away from their tent. Stan was terrified. He didn't have any clue as to what was out there. From the sound, it seemed like it was higher off the ground. Mentally, he estimated… eight feet? Nine feet? That couldn't be right, he thought. There was nothing in the area that stood anywhere near that tall. What the hell was it?

Whatever it was, there was absolutely no way he was getting out of that tent. Stan and his girlfriend huddled in the tent until the first rays of dawn began streaking across the landscape. After what was probably a very long and sleepless night, they packed their things as quickly as they could and left.

Several months later, the two settled in to watch some TV. As they turned through the stations, the couple settled on a show about unusual encounters involving large, ape-like creatures nicknamed Bigfoot. The encounters described on the program reminded them of their own encounter along the river that night. So many things seemed to fit, especially when they played a recording of one screaming that had been taken in the western United States. That roar on the television sounded uncannily like the one that they had heard.

Did Stan and his girlfriend have an encounter with Bigfoot that summer in 1989? Was a kind of missing link bellowing a challenge to someone for being on a part of the river that it had claimed as its own? Or did one of the documented animals that we know migrate through the area, such as a black bear, just happen to want to make its presence known as it made its way toward parts unknown?

Ultimately you, the reader, will have to be the judge.

THE SPIDER MONKEY SPECTER OF SYLVAN ISLAND

In late August 1923, the Rock Island Lines railroad company was preparing to accomplish an amazing, herculean feat. It was about to put into place the largest bridge girder that the world had ever seen.

The monstrous steel beam weighed nearly ninety-seven tons and stretched to 114 feet. It arrived in the Quad Cities by railroad, carried by three appropriately immense flatcars. The Rock Island Lines knew that it was going to be quite the spectacle, so it advertised the event in the local papers. The occasion was set for August 25. Specially designated trains carried people from all over Davenport, Rock Island and Moline to the site. Eventually, a crowd of three thousand people gathered to watch as two of the biggest cranes that many of them would probably ever see lifted the beam skyward.

Camera crews filmed, photographers snapped pictures and everyone held their breath as the giant girder was laid carefully into place between Arsenal Island and Moline, Illinois, at Sylvan Slough. According to historian Doug Smith, it would be "the longest and heaviest steel bridge girder ever laid across a stream in America."

While everyone celebrated a history-making event that day, only a short time before, the slough bore witness to something much grimmer. On

Sylvan Island Wagon Bridge on the Rock Island and Moline, Illinois border. The Mississippi River runs underneath it. *Photo by Bruce Walters.*

August 12, several men were fishing in the slough. One of them was Rosaris Carlino, a thirty-two-year-old Italian immigrant who worked in the ash pits at the People's Power Station in Moline. As he usually did on his work break, he went over to the slough to fish. No doubt the thought of his wife and baby crossed his mind as he walked along the shore. They were both still in Italy, but they would be joining him soon. He had never seen his son and was probably excited to finally lay eyes on him.

But as he walked, Carlino's foot slipped on a rock. Before he knew what was happening, he was falling into the water. Carlino couldn't swim. He struggled, trying desperately to find something to grab onto. He called out for help, but the other men who were there could only watch with a sick feeling in their stomachs. They couldn't swim either. After what must have seemed like an eternity, Carlino finally slipped beneath the water one last time.

Sylvan Slough, along with its namesake Sylvan Island, is an area that is no stranger to both triumph and tragedy. Originally, Sylvan Island was the tip of a peninsula that jutted out toward Arsenal Island directly to the north. It was a place where members of the Sauk and Meskwaki tribes wandered to fish, play and hunt. By 1832, they had been removed farther west, and white settlers gathered there instead.

From the beginning, local business interests wanted to better utilize the power of the Mississippi River. A prominent Moline businessman named David B. Sears had a dam built across Sylvan Slough that allowed water to be channeled to lumber mills on the riverfront. As the city grew, however, Sears's original dam began to cause problems. Perhaps chief among them was the fact that the openings that allowed water flow had been built too small. Not enough water could get through, and the river began to back up farther upstream, causing the water there to stagnate.

In the late 1860s, local officials entered into a deal with the federal government to build a massive new dam. This one had thirty-seven water gates that allowed for enough water to run the mills but also allowed the water to flow back into the river downstream.

By 1871, a broad channel had been cut through the peninsula that redirected the river water straight through to the mills. This channel severed thirty-eight acres from the tip of the peninsula, which was renamed Sylvan Island.

Nearly twenty years later, a hydroelectric power plant, the People's Light Company, was built. This plant provided electricity to the city of Davenport across the river. It was so successful that by 1900, the owners of the company were running the Moline Water Power Company as well.

The Sylvan Island Trail, which is 1.2 miles long, can be traveled by hiking or biking. *Photo by Bruce Walters.*

The industrial strength of the island grew rapidly at the turn of the century. In 1894, the Sylvan Steel Company constructed a steel mill there. A few years later, it was turned over to the Republic Iron and Steel Company, which primarily melted down steel rails and remade them into various parts to be used in mechanized agricultural equipment.

By the late 1950s, all of the industry on the island had been shut down and abandoned. Over the next decade, the ruins slowly faded into the increasingly dense natural growth on the island. But just because the island was deserted of people doesn't necessarily mean that there wasn't something there. Over the past few years, the Rock Island Paranormal group has conducted several paranormal investigations on Sylvan Island.

Lead investigator Ariel Renee Young said, "We did numerous investigations there. We have seen and encountered a full-bodied apparition that tends to take on several different forms. We have seen a full-uniformed Confederate soldier walking on the island. We heard audibly drums beating."

Other unusual phenomena include severe temperature changes. "It would be thirty degrees above zero and then our thermometers would drop fifty-four degrees below zero in certain other areas," Young said.

Right: The Sylvan Island Trail is teeming with trees, plants, wildflowers, various small animals and the remains of the old steel mill. *Photo by Bruce Walters*.

Below: The ruins of the old steel mill. *Photo by Bruce Walters.*

Rock Island Paranormal members also say that they have taken photographs on the island that show strange mists, as well as a mysterious shape that appeared to have first approached a member of their team before "passing through" the individual. "We have seen footprints in the snow that come from a tree, stop and then are not seen again. And had fully charged batteries just die," claimed Young.

One of the strangest experiences that Rock Island Paranormal encountered is that of the Spider Monkey Spirit. Ariel Renee Young, who claims to have seen the creature herself, said, "It looks like a spider monkey and goes flying from tree to tree to tree. It's dark, shadowy and flings through the trees. It doesn't stay in a place for very long. It doesn't want to stand still."

In her own experience, Young explained that sometimes all you see is a shadowy glimpse of the creature. You notice some leaves move and then some of the larger tree branches. "Then you turn the light off, you can see the shadow moving. And then you turn the light back on and nothing's there," she noted. "You hear creaking from the trees, see leaves falling. You shine a light up there, thinking it might be a squirrel or something like that. But you never see anything that had caused that noise."

It's hard to say what kind of monkey would—or could—live on the island. One theory about what it might be comes from the field of cryptozoology—the search for and study of animals whose existence or survival is disputed or unsubstantiated. Could there be a folkloric or mythical beast roaming the trees of Sylvan Island?

The island is home to a diverse group of wildlife, including several different species of mammals, fish and birds. Could it be that some kind of primate species also resides there, mostly hidden from visitors to the island? Is it possible that some kind of monkey species lives there, hiding from prying eyes? Or is it something more supernatural, like a ghost or some other kind of phantom being?

For those who might come into contact with the creature, Ariel Renee Young did offer some advice: "If you start smelling sulfur…you want to get out there, you want to start leaving immediately."

The Banshee of Brady Street

Brady Street is, and almost always has been, one of the main north–south roads that runs the length of the city of Davenport. It's an area that is

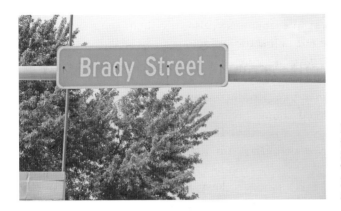

Brady Street sign on the corner of Brady Street and East Twenty-Ninth Street in Davenport, Iowa. *Photo by Michael McCarty.*

steeped in history yet still touches on the continued development and expansion of the city.

During the daylight hours, people swarm its length, busy going on whatever errands they have. After midnight, however, it is a different story.

The houses and businesses are dark, and the street itself empty. The harsh sodium glow of the streetlights burns holes in the gloom, the surrounding night made to seem all the much deeper for it. According to legend, that same gloom plays home to a creature straight out of Irish folklore.

The banshee is said to announce the impending death of a family member by letting out a piercing wail that chills whoever listens it to the center of their very soul. Anyone who has spent any amount of time on the streets of any city in the wee hours of the morning can attest to how eerily quiet it can be. To have that stillness pierced by a sound like that, seeming to come from everywhere and nowhere at the same time, would be disturbing to say the very least.

According to writer Jerome Pohlen, author of the book *Oddball Iowa*, our story begins with a man named Alfred Schacht. He, his wife and their two children moved into an old Victorian house along Brady Street in 1918. Soon, a series of tragic events unfolded for the family. The son was the first to go. The seven-year-old somehow fell from an attic window, landing on the fence below. The poor boy was run completely through by a fence post and died from his wounds. The daughter was the next to die, drowning in the bathtub.

The mother, Mrs. Schacht, was completely overwhelmed with grief. Unable to deal with the death of her two beloved children, she hanged herself in the house's basement. Alfred had nothing else to live for. Everyone he loved was gone. Following his wife's example, he hanged himself in the kitchen.

After the Schachts' tragic residence, no one wanted to buy the house. Some said that it was cursed, and there were probably others who just thought that a place where so much bad had happened just had a negative vibe to it.

Finally, a Chicago mobster bought the old house and turned it into a brothel. Business allegedly went pretty well. At least, until the first ghosts started to appear. Formerly faithful patrons suddenly found other things to do than spend their time in a haunted brothel.

It was during this time that the Banshee of Brady Street supposedly made her first appearance. It's unknown whose death her wail foretold at that first outing, but it did help kill business at the brothel for good. Later, it became a rooming house for local college students. Not surprisingly, the hauntings continued.

The tale of the Banshee of Brady Street is great. It makes for a wonderful telling on those gray, dreary days of October when the chill winds blow and the sunlight doesn't last quite as long as it did. Unfortunately, just because something makes for a good story doesn't mean that it's necessarily true.

Illustration by Jason McLean.

According to an article written by the researchers at the Richardson-Sloane Special Collections Center in 2008, there is no historical evidence that they could find that a family by the name of Schacht ever lived on Brady Street in 1918. To further complicate matters, there weren't any records showing that anyone by that name died between the years of 1917 and 1920.

Does that mean that the story is complete nonsense? The short answer is: maybe. As they point out, the lack of evidence supporting *that* particular origin story doesn't necessarily disprove that phenomenon ever took place. Even though someone saw a ghost, they might have gotten their backstory wrong.

The cursed home that saw so much tragedy and supernatural visitations is gone now; the ghosts said are to have moved into other places along Brady Street when the last wall fell. For all anyone knows, they might still be there. So, if you ever find yourself going along Brady Street in the wee hours of the morning, keep your eyes peeled in the dark and your ears open for a mournful wail…just in case.

Death Curve

The Legend of Julia Markham

A "dead man's curve," or "death curve," refers to a place where one or more fatal car accidents have taken place, usually around a nasty stretch of road. At some point, someone took the curve a little too fast, lost control of his or her car and died in the ensuing crash. Then, of course, the curve becomes cursed.

In Cambridge, Illinois, people tell a slightly different story. Their "death curve" is on a rural secondary road called Timber Line Road. For years, teenagers used to hang out in an old red barn that stood in that area. Although it's long gone now, it was a great place to get away from the prying eyes of their parents. There, among their peers, they could make their own poor decisions without too much judgment. A long time ago, something bad happened here. Something *really* bad. It started with a woman named Julia Markham.

Julia Johnson was about twenty-three years old when she married Clarence Markham. They settled into the modest farmhouse on the acreage that Clarence rented in Henry County, Illinois, and we can only imagine that they were very happy. A short time after their first wedding anniversary, they welcomed their first child, Clara, into the home. A year after that, they had a son, Harry. Clarence and Julia went on to have four more children after that: Charles, Mary, Lucy and their last, Asa, in 1905.

While Clarence and the children seem to have gone out and socialized with the other farm families in the area, Julia mostly kept to herself. Julia seemed to prefer spending the majority of her time with her family.

Illustration by Jason McLean.

Clarence was very laid-back and just allowed Julia to do what she was most comfortable with.

Like so many things in life, farm life is all about routine. From the time she was first married, Julia settled into hers. She mostly took care of chores around the house, like cooking and cleaning. The youngest children and the girls would have stayed under her watchful gaze, while the older boys would have been out working around the farm with their father.

And so it went, day after day, week after week, year after year. Routine can be excellent for efficiency, but one day starts to run into the next. There must have been a kind of dreary sameness to Julia's life, with very little to break up her schedule. Every day she was doing chores and taking care of small children, all the while dealing with must have seemed like a never-ending pregnancy. The Markhams were extremely poor, so even if they had the ability to attend the occasional dance or other event in town, they probably couldn't have paid for them anyway.

In July 1905, Clarence's father, Horace, came to visit. While he was staying there, Julia had a kind of mental breakdown and began to suffer from severe depression. The effect on her was more than enough for Clarence and Horace both to take notice. Horace was of the opinion that the daily drag and boredom of her daily routine was having a detrimental effect on his daughter-in-law.

Julia's depression continued unabated for the next several weeks. In mid-September 1905, her mother, Mary, was declared insane and taken to an asylum in Galesburg, Illinois. Julia's mental state grew worse. Clarence was concerned. He loved his wife, but he didn't know how to help her. Unfortunately, no one else really did either. Treatments that might have been considered for depression at that time included full immersion in water for extended periods of time, dietary changes and enemas. Clarence was helpless. All he could do was watch as his beloved Julia crumbled.

Julia was far worse off than anyone could have imagined. Trapped inside her own mind, Julia kept seeking her own solution to her problem. But her perception of the world was broken, perhaps even deranged. Having reached the absolute limits of her despair, Julia had come to a decisive conclusion about what she was going to do. After some planning, she sat down and wrote a private letter to her Clarence. She wanted to explain herself, so that he understood later. Julia placed it in a neighbor's mailbox, knowing that someone would find it eventually.

Putting on the best attitude she could muster, Julia told Clarence goodbye as he left that morning to go help out one of the other farmers with their harvest. The attitude change didn't alleviate his fears, however, and he was more worried than ever about his wife. He told his two eldest children, Clara and Harry, to stay home from school that day and keep an eye on their mother. With that, he left.

When people around the Markham farm saw the thick, black plumes of smoke billowing toward the powder blue sky on that calm autumn day in 1905, they immediately knew that something was wrong.

Several families left what they were doing and went to the Markhams'. As they approached, it was clear that the farmhouse was on fire, with flames leaping from the windows like a furnace. They rushed into the yard just in time to see Julia stumble out the front door. What remained of her clothing was on fire, and her exposed flesh had been badly burned. When they went to help her, they saw that she was also bleeding profusely from a horrendous gash in her neck.

While some of the men made an initial attempt to put out the fire, they quickly realized that the house was beyond saving. There was nothing to do but watch it burn.

Like everyone else, Clarence Markham had seen the smoke and come as quickly as he could. As soon as he got home, he began searching for his family. Clarence saw Julia, but not any of the children. Where were the children? With a lurching feeling in his stomach, he realized that they must still be inside the house.

As he began to sprint toward the door, some of the neighbors stopped him. He clawed and kicked and screamed like a wild animal, desperate to get to his little ones. But everyone knew that it was too late. Whoever was in that structure was already long past saving.

Sometime later, the county sheriff arrived, along with a local doctor and John Palmer, the chief of police in Cambridge. The sheriff began to question Julia about what had happened, while the doctor began to treat her wounds. As he sewed up the gash in her neck and did his best to treat her burns, the doctor realized that her wounds were fatal. Looking at the sheriff, he related the grim diagnosis.

According to Julia, a giant man with a great, black mustache and matching black hat had burst into the house. The stranger had an axe, which he had used to murder her children in front of her very eyes. He had then attacked her, slashing her across the throat. The sheriff didn't believe her. Neither did Palmer. Something about Julia's story just didn't add up. With time quickly ebbing away, they decided to get straight to the point. Palmer told Julia that they didn't believe her and to tell them the truth.

Julia was silent for a few moments and then asked what would happen to her if she did. Keeping it blunt, the sheriff told her that she was already dying. There wasn't much more that they could do to her. Taking a deep, ragged breath, Julia relaxed. As she began to speak, it seemed like a great weight was lifted off her shoulders.

Julia explained that she and the children had been eating watermelon that morning. When they finished, she asked Clara and Harry to fetch some water from the well. After they left, Julia used an axe to kill the other five children, none of whom were older than six.

When the eldest two returned, they were carrying a pail full of water between the two of them. Before they could react, Julia killed them too. Afterward, she carried each of them into her bedroom and laid them on the bed side by side. Then she soaked them and everything else with kerosene, lighting them on fire. Using the same knife that she had cut the watermelon with, she cut her own throat and then climbed into bed next to her children.

While Julia had planned to burn with them, something unexpected happened. As the flames quickly spread through the house, her survival instincts kicked in. Julia got out of bed and slowly made her way through the smoke to the front door. As she finished, Julia's voice trailed off, and she died just a few moments later.

Everyone was stunned. They couldn't believe that this had happened. Clarence was almost incoherent with grief. But there was nothing he, or anyone else, could do. His entire family was gone in the span of just a few hours.

A short time later, a rural mail carrier found the letter that Julia had left for Clarence. Addressed to Clarence, it said, "Dear Clarence: This is to say good-by to you. Some give their souls for others, and I will do this for my children. God bless them! They will all die happy in the arms of Jesus. I will meet them there, and some day you will join us, too."

They say that Julia Markham still haunts the road out here, especially around the curve. They say that she appears out of nowhere and causes people to die when they wreck their cars. The true story behind the Markham family tragedy was largely forgotten over the years. What people remembered of it gradually distorted into a kind of urban legend.

Julia and all of her children were buried at nearby Rose Dale Cemetery. The remains of the children were buried in one casket, while Julia's were interred in another right next to them. Both the graves were unmarked.

Some newspaper accounts claimed that Clarence, so crushed by his grief, committed suicide in a truly dramatic fashion. Not wanting to live anymore, Clarence had allegedly put a noose around his neck and then shot himself. As his body fell, the rope pulled tight, guaranteeing that if he survived the gunshot, he would definitely die by strangulation. While this was certainly very dramatic, Clarence never committed suicide. Soon after they reported it, the papers printed retractions. He remarried almost a decade later, passing away at the age of seventy-seven in 1951.

The house was never rebuilt. The ruins were plowed under, leaving virtually no physical sign that the tragedy had ever taken place. The only thing to show that there had ever been a farm there at all was the big red barn.

At some point, the ghost stories began. Locals began to claim that the ghost of Julia Markham could be seen at what had become known as the "Cambridge Death Curve." While easy to dismiss as part of the already popular legend, there are people around Cambridge who truly believe that the curve is haunted.

According to one account, two women spotted something strange as they drove toward the curve one night. There, in the corn field, was a white shape, with what seemed to be long hair floating out behind it like it was underwater. Others have also claimed to see the white figure, presumed by some to be the spirit of Julia Markham, searching for the children she murdered more than 115 years ago. Former Henry County sheriff Gilbert Cady claims that according to local legend, the spirit of Julia Markham is supposed to appear every September 25 on the site of her old property. Still others claim to have seen ghostly lights in the area.

Does the spirit of Julia Markham still haunt the site of the tragedy that she caused so long ago? Or are the ghostly sightings the product of overwrought imaginations? Whatever the truth behind the haunting, there is no doubt that a horrific tragedy took place there that claimed the lives of eight people. Julia Markham, in many ways, really was haunted—a prisoner of her own mental illness. No matter how much those close to her wanted to help, there was little they could do.

While the legend of the "Cambridge Death Curve" serves as a cautionary tale to take care when approaching potentially dangerous sections of roads, the true story of Julia Markham provides another truth: sometimes the most dangerous spirits are the ones called up within the confines of your own mind.

Chippiannock Cemetery

The Chippiannock Cemetery is located at 2901 Twelfth Street in Rock Island, Illinois. The need for Chippiannock first arose in 1854. Rock Island had a population of about five thousand people then, and the dead were being buried somewhat haphazardly in a local pasture, roughly where Longview Park is now.

In 1855, Chippiannock's founders purchased sixty-two acres on Manitou Ridge and secured the services of noted landscape architect Almerin Hotchkiss to design the cemetery in the rural cemetery style of Mount Auburn in Massachusetts, America's first garden-style cemetery.

The graveyard was listed in the National Register of Historic Places on May 6, 1994. It was the first cemetery in Illinois to be listed in the National Register. It is a pivotal location in Max Allan Collins's graphic novel *Road to Perdition*, which was turned into a major motion picture starring Tom Hanks, Paul Newman and Jude Law.

Chippiannock Cemetery: Epitaphs Brought to Life was a one-day performance in the graveyard by local actors portraying historical figures buried there. Michael McCarty's grandmother Ann Burdt was

Chippiannock Cemetery is located at 2901 Twelfth Street in Rock Island, Illinois. Its name means "Village of the Dead" in the native dialect of the Sauk and Meskwaki tribes. *Photo by Michael McCarty.*

one of the actresses who performed there during the 1990s. Chippiannock's name means "Village of the Dead" in the native dialect of the Sauk and Meskwaki tribes.

Over the next 164 years, hundreds of people would come to know the cemetery as their final earthly abode. Some of them were rich and some of them poor, but all of them had a story. The following are a few notable standouts.

THE GRAVE ROBBER AND THE TIFFANY STAINED GLASS

Frederick C.A. "Carl" Denkmann was known as an individual who went from journeyman machinist to "one of the most prominent lumber men in the world." According to Minda Powers-Douglas, author of *Chippiannock Cemetery* (Images of America), Denkmann and his wife, Catherine, emigrated from Germany and eventually settled in Rock Island in 1851. "He was business partners with Frederick Weyerhauser, who was married to Catherine's sister, Sarah. The Weyerhauser-Denkmann Lumber Company was king of the lumber mills. At their peak, they owned four mills and output 117 million feet of white pine lumber per year."

After the Denkmanns passed away, they were buried at a mausoleum in Chippiannock. The mausoleum had a Tiffany memory window made of stained glass called the "River of Life." "The window was made in 1905," Powers-Douglas said. "Louis Comfort Tiffany was the creator and designer." The window overlooked the final resting place of the Denkmanns for decades—its undisturbed beauty untarnished. On the morning of April 5, 1976, that all changed.

While conducting his rounds of the cemetery, Joseph Vogele, the superintendent at Chippiannock, discovered a gaping hole where the "River of Life" window should have been. He immediately went back to the office and called the police.

Even though the Rock Island police thoroughly investigated the theft, they couldn't find anything. At one point, the FBI even got involved. Unfortunately, it didn't have any more luck than the local police had. "It was a possibility it was part of a grave robbing ring that was going on in the 1970s, when a number of places all over the United States were robbing Victorian era, early 1920s era [graves]," said Powers-Douglas.

Above: The mausoleum where Frederick C.A. "Carl" Denkmann and Catherine Denkmann were buried. *Photo by Michael McCarty.*

Left: The "River of Life" stained-glass window was stolen from the Denkmann Mausoleum in 1976. *Photo by Bruce Walters.*

Opposite: The "River of Life" stained-glass window was created and designed by Louis Comfort Tiffany. *Photo by Bruce Walters.*

For years, the window stayed missing. Eventually, Joseph Vogele retired from his position as superintendent. His son, Greg, took over soon after. The theft of the "River of Life" had always bothered him, and he was determined to find out what had happened to it. Greg began to send out letters to auction houses, museums and places known to have Tiffany windows in them. The thieves had taken the window intact, strongly suggesting that they were aware of its value. That meant that if they hadn't been collectors keeping for themselves, they would probably try to sell it. One of these venues might have seen the window and remembered who the seller had been.

It took twenty years, but Greg Vogele finally found the lead he was looking for. The Charles Morse Museum of American Art in Winter Park, Florida, sent him a letter saying that they had an idea where the "River of Life" could be found.

As it turned out, a couple in the New York City area had purchased the window from sellers in the state of Colorado. At first, they were absolutely adamant that their window wasn't stolen. To settle the question, the FBI stepped in once again. The piece was thoroughly tested and examined by one of the bureau's specialized divisions, which vetted its authenticity. Finally, the lost window had been found.

"They got the River of Life back in 1997. In 1999 they had the crack fixed. They didn't want it to be in an unsafe place like inside a mausoleum," Powers-Douglas said. "They had it displayed for years at the Davenport Museum of Art, then it went into storage for a while." Later, they made a special exhibit for the window and placed it on permanent display. "It is beautiful, it is a stunning piece."

Thanks to the dogged determination of Greg Vogele, everyone who visits the Figge Art Museum can enjoy this long-lost piece of Quad City history.

THE MAD BUTCHER OF MILAN

It was February 1896 in Milan, Illinois. The cold had long since set in, and people were dealing with it as best they could. But Fredrick Kuschmann was dead. He had fallen off his horse, struck his head and died. Only twenty-one years old, his life was cut short in its prime. His family, however, didn't believe that it was an accident. There was something about his death that they didn't like, but they just couldn't quite put their finger on it. They were determined to get to the bottom of it.

According to authorities, Kuschmann was found lying along the side of the road by Henry Bastian, a local farmer and Kuschmann's boss. Bastian claimed that he found the young man, who was obviously hurt, and immediately went to get a doctor.

The county coroner ruled the death an accident, Kuschmann having been thrown from a skittish horse and hitting his head. The family, having none of it, put enough pressure on local law enforcement that an investigation was opened.

Illustration by Jason McLean.

According to Bastian, Kuschmann had put in his notice after fulfilling the terms of a year-long employment contract at his farm. The farmer paid Kuschmann right away and made arrangements for him to collect his belongings from the farm the next day.

Like the family, investigators had reason to believe that all was not as it seemed. "His head was severely bruised," Minda Powers-Douglas said. "There were no other signs of trauma to the body. It didn't fit with him being thrown from a horse, unless the horse picked him up, put him down and hit him. This [didn't] seem right."

When they examined the evidence from the scene of Kuschmann's death, they noted that his coat had been found near the body and was covered in blood. Also, there was no money found on his body, even though he had just gotten paid. They theorized that Kuschmann had been attacked and robbed. His murderer had then wrapped the young man's head in his own coat and dumped the body.

Figuring that a completely random attack was unlikely, the police were left with only one suspect: Henry Bastian. They theorized that Bastian killed Kuschmann so that he wouldn't have to pay anything. The farmer then wrapped Kuschmann's head in his own coat to help prevent any blood getting on anything. Finally, he dumped the body and then went for help, making the whole incident seem like a tragic accident.

When the authorities contacted Bastian's mother, they discovered that Henry had forged his parents' names on the mortgage for the farm five years earlier and that he had recently defaulted on the mortgage. Just when police thought they were zeroing in on a suspect, Bastian's body was found hanging in his granary. Whatever justice he was facing would now have to come from a higher authority.

WHILE KUSCHMANN'S MURDER WAS evidently solved, locals began to talk about other young hired hands who had seemingly disappeared from the Bastian farm. Police began to wonder, too, and eventually tracked down a former employee of Bastian's, Charles Reiher, and questioned him about the disappearances.

According to Reiher, he had seen Bastian burying a body on the farm. A former mental patient, Reiher was afraid that people would just think that he was crazy and not believe him. Armed with this information, police received permission to start looking for a body on the Bastian farm. They found the remains of two more former employees, both seemingly murdered. "Henry Bastian was buried on March 15th, 1896 in an unmarked grave at Chippiannock Cemetery," Powers-Douglas said. "And one of his victims was buried in an unmarked grave too."

Premonitions of Doom

John F. Dillon stood, inspecting the monument in front of him. He stared up at the granite obelisk, remembering his wife and children, the love and laughter that they had shared. But his memories of his wife and eldest daughter were always tinged with sadness now. Dillon couldn't help but remember that as much as it represented such a wonderful part of his life, the monument also was a constant, deliberate reminder of the greatest loss that he had ever known.

John was born in New York in 1831. While he was still a boy, his family moved west to Davenport, Iowa, in 1838. At seventeen, John started training under the watchful eye of one of the most accomplished doctors in the area. A year later, he began attending medical school, earning his medical degree in 1850. However, after a short practice, John realized that he wasn't cut out to be a doctor.

Returning to Davenport, Dillon followed the advice of a friend and began to study law. By 1852, John had applied for and was granted admittance to the Scott County bar, becoming a full-fledged lawyer. Within a year, he was elected prosecuting attorney for Scott County, Iowa, and by the late 1850s, he was a judge of the Seventh Judicial District of Iowa. During this time, John began writing books on the law. Royalties from these books eventually made him a small fortune. Dillon continued to excel and was elected to the Iowa Supreme Court in 1863.

In 1869, he was appointed the circuit judge for the Eighth Judicial Circuit of the United States, placing seven states under his watchful eye. After a stellar

The Dillon Memorial is a historic structure located in LeClaire Park, in downtown Davenport, Iowa. New York artists Franklin and Arthur Ware designed the memorial in association with Paul Schultz. The Dillon Memorial is a Neoclassical structure built in concrete and is commonly referred to as the "Dillon Fountain." *Photo by Michael McCarty.*

career, Dillon retired from active practice ten years later. With his extensive knowledge of the law, he was offered a position as a law professor at Columbia University in New York City. It was a fantastic opportunity, and he readily accepted. John and his family packed up their belongings and moved east.

He married Anna Price, the daughter of a prominent Davenport politician, in 1853. She was strong-willed and intelligent, every inch his equal. Anna loved art and music and was a well-known philanthropist. John adored her. Settling comfortably into their life in New York, John worked as Anna began an annual tradition of going to Europe for extended vacations.

In 1890, their eldest daughter, Annie, got married. The ceremony was held in the Dillons' home on Madison Avenue, followed by a beautiful reception. Unfortunately, the union was an extremely unhappy one, and the couple soon divorced. Annie moved back in with her parents and became her mother's traveling companion on her European vacations.

In 1898, Anna was really looking forward to one of her trips, despite being in ill health. She felt that a visit to some of the mineral baths in Europe would help her feel better. This time, Anna also wanted a change of pace from the usual travel company she booked with. After some looking, Anna decided to arrange passage with a very reputable and reliable French company.

Shortly before she was due to leave, John began to feel uneasy about his wife's trip. Usually, he was accustomed to long absences from his wife and children. For them, extended trips were part and parcel of their lives, and so they probably didn't think much of them leaving. He had broken his leg in late 1897 and had been bedridden for quite a while as it healed. It would be good for him to get away from the house while Anna and Annie went overseas.

Still, Dillon's horrible feeling of impending doom just would not go away. No matter how much he tried to rationalize his feelings, he couldn't shake the idea that something bad was going to happen on that trip. John reminded himself that he didn't believe in premonitions or portents, yet his sense of dread only intensified. It bothered him so much that he finally asked Anna to postpone the trip until the fall. She wasn't any more a believer than he was, and she told John that everything would be fine. Nothing bad was going to happen. How many times had she taken this trip before? She'd always come back to him, safe and sound.

Besides, the ship had a reliable reputation. It had made the trip back and forth between New York and Europe for years with very few problems. All would be well. John and Anna had been married for forty years, and he knew when he was defeated. Reluctantly, he conceded her point and quit arguing, despite his persistent feelings.

On July 2, 1898, John escorted his Anna and Annie to the pier, joined by his wife's nurse and daughter's maid, to see them off on their voyage. They lovingly said their goodbyes and parted ways. John took out his handkerchief and waved to them from the pier as their ship pulled out and began to make its way toward the open ocean. He watched as his beloved wife and daughter faded into the distance, waving their own handkerchiefs to him from the promenade deck.

John Dillon had been a professional lawyer longer than some people had been alive in 1898. He was an intelligent and persuasive man. But as he stood at the end of that New York City pier that day, nothing could help him shake the feeling that something awful was about to happen.

La Bourgogne was a French steamship that had successfully navigated the Atlantic waters between France and New York for a decade. It was fast and dependable. If asked, a good many people might have recommended it for travel before it departed that July day in 1898. About 720 other people were on board with the Dillon entourage, including the crew. The ship was in excellent condition, and for the first two days, it made steady progress north toward Canada before veering east toward Europe.

In the early morning hours of July 4, 1898, *La Burgogne* was traveling off of Nova Scotia through thick, heavy fog. The ship was moving fast in spite of the low visibility. Without warning, the steamer collided with the *Cromartyshire*, a British ship that was also making its way through the area.

La Bourgogne severely damaged the *Cromartyshire*, tearing off its bow as well as doing damage to the deck. After a quick inspection, the British vessel's crew determined that their ship wasn't going to sink and so went to work on clearing the wreckage caused by the collision. As they worked, they heard the steamer's whistle blow, which they answered with their fog horn. A short time later, the crew saw a signal rocket launch from the French ship, followed by a shot. Once again, the *Cromartyshire* answered in kind, sending up its own rockets. This time, there was no response. The crew went back to work, unaware of the events that were unfolding aboard *La Bourgogne*.

The collision with the *Cromartyshire* had torn a ten-foot gash in the starboard side of the steamer. It was so early in the morning that most of the passengers were still asleep below decks at the time. Some were able to sleep through it, while others, awoken by the crash, rushed to the main deck. The ship had been mortally wounded, and nearly everyone who was there in that moment knew it.

A.D. LaCasse, a language professor from New Jersey, was one of those on deck when the collision took place. He quickly ran below to his cabin and woke up his wife. Together, they returned to the deck, ready to follow orders to evacuate. Others had done the same, and the decks were soon crowded with frightened passengers.

The captain had blown the ship's whistle and sent up the signal rocket after the collision in an effort to contact anyone who might be in the area for help. He and some of the officers stood on the deck, shouting orders at the crew to get passengers into the lifeboats and lower them safely into the water. The sailors mostly ignored them, seemingly frozen in place. Then, in one stunning surge, all hell broke loose.

Although later reports contradicted one another, several eyewitnesses saw the crew man lifeboats without helping anyone else. Others said that passengers from steerage crowded around the boats, preventing the crew from doing their jobs.

Some watched as *La Bourgogne*'s second officer tried his best to free lifeboats from where they were tied or chained to the ship. He ran from boat to boat, working desperately to work free as many as he could. Some passengers tried to do the same, seeking to lower people safely into the water. Several of the passengers boarded lifeboats that were still connected to the ship, waiting patiently for one of the crew to lower them. Some of the men tried their best to free the boats themselves. A few managed, but many more were stranded.

Many crew members were trapped below decks as water poured into the ship. These men tried to save the ship, but as soon as the water put out the fires in the boilers that powered the vessel, they knew that all was lost. The last time the captain was ever seen, he was on the bridge, apparently having lost all control, waving his arms around, screaming and shouting at someone.

Through it all, the ship continued to list to the starboard side as it sank slowly into the Atlantic. As it did, it became harder for people to maintain their footing on the slanting deck. Some of the people in lifeboats still lashed to the ship were dumped out into the water below, unable to stay inside.

With little choice, others jumped as *La Bourgogne* began its final descent into the water. The suction caused by the vessel was immense as it slipped below the waves, pulling everyone and everything down with it. Survivors tried desperately to swim away, fighting against the awful pull. Among those struggling in the water was A.D. LaCasse's wife. She had slid from the deck as the ship's list had become so extreme that she could no longer keep her footing. Thankfully, she was wearing a life jacket, which helped her to say afloat.

She and her husband became separated in the crush of people on the deck, but she had no time to worry about that now. She swam as hard as she could to get away from the dying *La Bourgogne*. She later remembered being surrounded by desperate and drowning passengers—children, women and men—screaming in terror as they were sucked under the water. As she swam, something bumped hard into her, pushing her away from the whirlpool and into calmer water. Almost before she knew it, someone roughly seized her arm and dragged her into a lifeboat. Looking to see who her rescuer was, she was both astonished and relieved to see her husband holding on to her. She didn't know it yet, but Mrs. A.D. LaCasse was the only female passenger to live through the disaster.

Others were not so lucky. In what would be the most controversial testimony to come from *La Bourgogne* disaster, several people testified to horrifying acts of cruelty on the part of the ship's crew. According to some, many of the crew sought to save themselves by getting on available lifeboats and cutting them free before *La Bourgogne* actually sank. Allegedly, they guarded them with ruthless efficiency.

In the water, people tried to survive any way they could. Some swam, while others clung to makeshift rafts. Some had managed to board lifeboats. There were many who tried to climb into the boats from the frigid water, desperate to survive. To their shock, the ruthless and callous people who were already in the boats threw them back into the water to die. Men and women alike were assailed with oars and boathooks. Some were bludgeoned to death by iron bars or oars, while others were pushed under the water to drown.

One man survived by clinging onto the lifeline of one of the boats. As he held on for his very life, he was forced to watch as his mother, a short distance away, was pushed under the waves with oars by the lifeboat passengers as she tried to climb into their boat.

Charles Liebra had put his two sons on board a lifeboat before the ship sank. Liebra himself went into the water with *La Burgogne*, and when he surfaced, he could not find his sons. Desperately, he tried to climb into a passing lifeboat, only to be beaten black and blue by those on board. Back into the water he went, staying afloat any way possible before he was rescued. His sons were never found.

As the men on the *Cromartyshire* made their repairs, they were able to make out two lifeboats coming toward them. Quickly discovering the fate of the steamer that had struck them, the crew of the British vessel went out and began rescuing as many people as they could. Out of the 725 on board *La Burgogne*, only 163 survived, making it one of the worst maritime disasters of that era.

When he received the phone call informing him of the disaster, John Dillon was crushed. For days, he'd been worried about Anna and Annie. That feeling of impending disaster just wouldn't go away and was never fully out of his thoughts. Now, the horrible premonition that had haunted him for so long had finally come true.

As news about the disaster trickled in, Dillon held out hope that perhaps his wife and daughter were still on board a lifeboat that hadn't been found yet. If they were still adrift, then they might yet be rescued. As time passed, however, the awful truth gradually sank in, and hope was replaced by a simple desire to bring their bodies home for burial.

Dillon, along with another man who had lost family in the disaster, hired a ship and went out to the Atlantic, hoping to recover their remains. After ten days, they gave up. Their bodies, like so many others, were never recovered, claimed forever by the jealous Atlantic. Dillon returned to his home in New York, now all the drearier for the absence of his beloved family.

After an investigation, shipping company authorities claimed that the crew of *La Bourgogne* performed heroically during the disaster. They manned their stations and followed orders, only abandoning ship when told to do so by their superiors. They also claimed that, according to eyewitness testimony, it was steerage passengers who were to blame for the immense loss of life. They panicked when the ship began to list and blocked the crew from doing their jobs and getting people in the boats or cutting free those that they could. Shipping authorities also claimed that some boats weren't able to be freed because of the listing of *La Bourgogne* as it sank.

Addressing the claims that crew members had deliberately prevented people from getting on board rafts by hitting them with oars, the shipping company claimed that the crew was acting in the interests of the survivors on the boat. Already overloaded, one more passenger would cause the raft to capsize, more than likely killing twenty or thirty people. The one was sacrificed for the greater good.

Some believed, some didn't. In the end, it didn't matter. The investigation, as far as the authorities were concerned, was over. The survivors were left to mourn their lost loved ones and live with whatever horrible things they had seen or done.

Although his friends were worried that the shock of losing his wife and daughter would kill him, John endured. The memory of his Anna and Annie was always with him, and he eventually commissioned the monument at Oakdale Cemetery to stand as an eternal memorial to not only them, but also to all the other lives lost on *La Burgoyne*.

Dillon had never experienced any kind of premonitions before July 1898, nor did he report any after. Whether it was some kind of divine inspiration, psychic flash or something else entirely, the "why" of the incident is open to speculation. Whatever it was, Dillon had taken heed. He had tried but was ultimately unable to avert the fate of his loved ones. In the end, there was nothing more for him to do but carry on and mourn the dead.

Dillon had made sure that their memory and the disaster that claimed their lives would be forever etched in stone. And even though he couldn't save them or be buried near their earthly remains, he saw to it that his memory and theirs would be close to each other for the rest of time. Perhaps, in death, John F. Dillon was able to learn the truth behind his strange and dark premonitions in the summer of 1898.

The Giant of Scott County

If you were to peruse a history of the small town of Long Grove, Iowa, you are very likely to find a very interesting black-and-white photograph. In it stands a huge man, looking at the camera with relative disinterest. The viewer can't help but notice the man's size. Yes, he's very overweight, but he also has an enormous frame for it to hang on. The picture definitely gives the impression that the man is truly gigantic.

Giants are the stuff of legend. Generally portrayed to be huge creatures, they occupy prominent places in legends and fairy tales. Although imaginary, there occasionally comes along a person who has extraordinary qualities that make others compare them with such creatures. William Orndorff—or Bill, as he was more commonly known—was such a man. While his tremendous girth earned him a place in the annals of eastern Iowa history, there was much more to the man than the nickname that became synonymous with his legend: "Fatty."

Bill was born near Long Grove, Iowa, in 1875. By all accounts, his childhood was relatively normal. He played, worked and socialized like other children and grew up comfortably on his family's farm. Tall and good-looking, Bill had a lovely singing voice and was known as a good dancer. He was also charming and well-liked by nearly everyone. And then he got sick—at least, that's what his family claimed. They said that Bill caught something that no friend or doctor could identify. While he made a full recovery, he started gaining weight shortly after. Before long, Bill weighed about four hundred pounds. That didn't bother him too much, though, and if it did, he didn't let it show. He remained a very friendly, approachable person.

He still loved to go to dances, where he would often serve as a caller and would even occasionally step out onto the floor. Never a particularly shy man, Bill was known to shout at passersby to come and join the festivities.

Orndorff was also known for being immensely strong. For several years, he worked at the Meier Implement Company in Long Grove. One of his primary duties there was to assemble horse-drawn agricultural equipment. These were made primarily out of cast iron and steel, designed for rugged outdoor use. As such, many of the components were very heavy. There were some pieces that required the use of two men—one to hold the piece while the other fastened it into place. Bill was so strong that he could do all of it by himself, simply holding it with one hand while putting it on with the other.

To entertain themselves, Orndorff and his boss, who was also known as being very strong, would hold foot races between the hills outside the shop. But first, they would strap themselves into pieces of farm equipment where the horse would normally be hooked up and then race from the top of one hill to the next, pulling the equipment behind them.

Giants are expected to be strong. However, they're not expected to be quick. At more than four hundred pounds, most didn't figure that Bill could move very fast. In spite of his girth, however, Bill had lost none of his youthful agility. Of course, most of the locals knew about Bill's impressive talents, and they used them to their full advantage. Sooner or later, someone from out of town would stop into the local bar that Bill frequented. When they came in, the bartender would start an act that he had already worked out with Bill beforehand.

Approaching the stranger, he would point to Bill and ask, "You see that guy?" Bill was very hard to miss.

"Sure," the stranger replied.

"You know, I've seen him kick the pipe off the top of that stove," the bartender said, pointing to a cast-iron stove in the corner. Inevitably, the stranger would scoff at the claim. Bill was massive, and the pipe was about six feet from the floor. There was no way that guy was going to kick that pipe from its place. None. And the stranger said so. The two men would commence to debating the issue, and at some point, the bartender would offer to bet cold hard cash that he was right.

The stranger—fueled by a lethal combination of righteous indignation, outright anger and just a little booze—would take it. Now that he had his prey firmly on the hook, the bartender would yell at Bill and tell him about the bet. Bill would then get up and make a huge production of warming up, lining up his kick and a bunch of other nonsense. The theatrics made it so much more fun when he would throw his foot up in the air and kick the pipe off the stove with little effort. Everyone would have a good laugh and have a drink, generally at the stranger's expense.

Through it all, Bill never stopped gaining weight. The last time that he allowed himself to be weighed, he was more than four hundred pounds. He became known throughout the region for his size, and some even started to call him the "Giant of Scott County."

As he approached middle age, the excess weight began to take a toll on Bill. He couldn't get around very well, and so he moved to a farm northeast of Long Grove, where he paid the owners to help take care of him. Outside of being extremely overweight, Bill enjoyed relatively good health. His size was slowing him down, but he was still as friendly as ever. He could still talk and visit, and he hadn't gotten sick in years. But all of that was about to change.

The Great War—what people would later call World War I—was in full swing, with much of the world in the throes of combat in various parts of the globe. The United States had just entered the conflict the year before. Thousands of young men gathered at camps around the country to be equipped and trained before shipping out to fight the scourge of the German Hun on the fields Europe. And that was part of the problem.

In later years, scientists would debate where it all started. Some said China and others Europe. Today, the consensus is that it started on the wheat-covered plains of Kansas. A group of men in Kansas left their camp carrying an unseen threat, one that no one knew was there. Traveling laborers in China carried it, taking it to their family, friends and neighbors. As they went from place to place, so did the silent menace, quickly taking root among a populace that was almost completely unprepared for it. Before long, it had spread around the world.

Although its effects were already begin seen in several places, the newspapers in Spain were the first to report about it. Because they were the first to talk about it, the world gave it their name: the Spanish influenza.

Some of the first cases in Iowa were reported at Camp Dodge in Des Moines, Iowa, where hundreds of soldiers had become infected. Medical officials told the public to wear cloth masks—little more than handkerchiefs tied over the face—to help slow the spread of the disease. As it had throughout the world, the Spanish flu spread quickly throughout the state. It was indiscriminate in who it struck. World leaders caught it, as did the governor of Iowa, who was running for reelection at the time. Students and professors caught it at the University of Iowa and Iowa State College.

In 1918, there was little that doctors could do to fight the Spanish flu. The discovery of penicillin was still nearly thirty years away, so medical professionals could often do little more than separate the sick from the healthy. In an effort to do that, public places ranging from schools to movie theaters were closed. Many public events, such as religious services and sporting events, were either canceled or closed off to all but a few people. Still the disease spread, virtually unchecked.

That year, the Spanish influenza brought the world to its knees. Sometimes people got lucky and didn't get sick, but others, like Bill, found that their luck had run out. Inside of his rented room in northern Scott County, Iowa, the physically resilient man was laid low with the flu. Millions of people around the world were in the same situation. The virus affected their lungs, gradually breaking them down. As they did, the victims' lungs would begin to fill with blood, causing many of them to cough up blood as their bodies tried to expel the fluid. As their immune systems weakened, many of the sick caught pneumonia.

In December, Bill joined the thousands of Iowans who succumbed to the ravages of the Spanish flu. He was only forty-three years old. Some say that when they removed him from his home, they had to cut a hole in the side of the house. An autopsy was performed, and when the coroner weighed him, Bill weighed a little more than seven hundred pounds.

Years prior, many of his family had moved to Clinton County, only about ten miles to the north of the Long Grove area. Because of this, it was decided that the funeral would be held in DeWitt, a centrally located town for all of his family and friends. A specially built casket was ordered for him, one that could accommodate his enormous size. Some have said that his coffin was actually two piano boxes that were put together. Regardless, a casket was found, and the funeral was held without any issues.

When the services were concluded, it took twelve men to load Bill onto a flatbed truck. The truck was necessary because he wouldn't fit into a normal hearse. The funeral procession then made its way south to Mount Joy Cemetery, on the northern limits of the city of Park View.

At the grave site, a block and tackle was used to lift Bill from the truck and into the ground. His grave was marked with a small, simple stone that stood in sharp contrast to the huge man buried below. He had so many talents that he had used for the benefit and entertainment of others while asking very little in return.

Bill Orndorff was a living legend, and he lived life to the fullest way that he knew how. But in 1918, a silent killer swept through the world and took

The tombstone of William Orndorff, who weighed more than four hundred pounds. He became known throughout the region for his size, and some even called him the "Giant of Scott County." The Mount Joy Cemetery is located in Long Grove, Iowa. *Photo by Michael McCarty.*

that life away from him. In the end, a legendary illness brought down the legendary giant.

Many of the things that Bill would have known and recognized are gone now, torn down or replaced over the one hundred years since his death. And yet his story and life are still remembered, passed down through the generations as something that truly stood out and was special. In that way, Bill Orndorff, the Giant of Scott County, remains with us still, humbly tucked away among our collective rural Iowa lore, ready to tell his fantastic story from his simple resting place near Park View, Iowa.

UFO Sightings

According to the National UFO Reporting Center, there have been nearly one hundred sightings in the Quad City Area just since the year 2000.

Beverly Trout from Perry, Iowa—who was with Mutual UFO Network, Iowa (MUFON), for nearly three decades but became an independent UFO investigator in 2020—gave an exclusive interview for this book. She has carried out hundreds of investigations and reports for MUFON and on her own.

"The number of 'reports' has nothing to do with the actual number of sightings, since many witnesses do not report," Trout said. "Theoretically there could have been 500 or 1,000. Nor are installations a factor, though UFOs can at times appear near such locations. Bottom line is UFOs are apt to appear anywhere, depending upon their agenda on those occasions, i.e. physical face-to-face encounters with witnesses, sometimes checking earth installations, most of the time influencing what's taking place and how the witness perceives it."

In the 1970s, there were crop circles that appeared in Milan and led to reports in the local newspapers and on the local news. There were rumors of cattle mutilations in the area but nothing substantial. Trout continued:

> I have not heard of any cattle mutilations in the Quad Cities. I handled a case that happened in Iraq in 2005 re: mutilation of 37 female dogs. In 1998, I was asked to go to southeastern South Dakota to interview

Illustration by Jason McLean.

farmers who had lost an 1800 lb. bull—bull evidently had been dropped straight down onto three strands of barbed wire fence, no tracks, no blood. A cow had been mutilated a half mile away. Coyotes would not touch either animal. Farmers that night had also had actual sightings of UFOs.

I specialize in abduction/experiencer cases, and I should emphasize that there are many happening all the time all over the state. So, undoubtedly, there have been many in the Quad Cities Area that have never been reported to me. Such witnesses are, more often than not, reluctant to report their experiences to an organization, and may not know they can report to someone like me who will not reveal their identity to the public. However, I have in the past, and am currently, handling many such non-organizational reports as an independent researcher.

There was an alien abduction incident in the Quad Cities area:

I did handle an abduction case that occurred in the Davenport area in 1997. Three young men were driving from Kansas City to Chicago, and when they got to Davenport at 10:00 p.m., a bright pulsating white light surrounded their car, pulsated for a few seconds before it disappeared. The three of them talked about it for a few minutes, and noted they couldn't see any other lights for miles in any direction. When they arrived in Chicago, they were surprised to find that it was 3:00 a.m. instead of their expected arrival time of 1:00 a.m.—Missing time of two hours. *A few weeks later the reporting witness had a cold and went to the doctor. Checking his ears, the doctor noticed an object and pulled it out (a painful process). Object was dull grey metallic color, covered with blood and tissue and about the size of small marble. Incidentally, the witness in question later became an attorney.*

An interesting case happened in southern Iowa. The young man witness was standing in his parents' cow pasture on a bright sunny day, no clouds in the sky, when there came a shadow over his head. He looked up to see hovering at only 100 feet altitude a huge silent triangle, estimated at 600 feet on each side. At first, he was horrified. Next thing he knew, he was located about 100 feet away, down on one knee, still looking up at the triangle, but now he was no longer frightened. *Obviously, some element of interaction had taken place. Certainly, the witness' psychological reaction had been influenced/manipulated to take away his fear.*

Beverly Trout is also an abductee/experiencer, with ongoing UFO activity—this helps her to establish a comfortable zone of communication when she's asked to interact in dialogue with witnesses who have face-to-face experiences.

I've been taken since early childhood. I've even had a couple conscious encounters when traveling out of state. And of course, it has long been known that UFO occupants have no problem in locating those with whom they interact, whether they're at their home location or elsewhere. I do not make a big issue of my own experiences when speaking before audiences within Iowa, but I have spoken at conferences around the country, and have done many radio interviews around the country, so it is known in the public that I am an "experiencer." I just don't make an issue of it if I'm teaching classes on UFOs, or speaking. However, I do a lot of Q&A, so if I'm asked if I'm involved, I give a truthful answer, but I also give a minimal answer because I'd like an audience to focus on the main topic of UFOs and the alien ETs who are interacting with so many on the planet, so I try to keep audiences focused on the cases that demonstrate the facts (as far as we know them) regarding UFOs.

Her last words on the subject are these:

I've mentioned hybrids that I've known—some of them for many years. They're just generally nice people, most of them showing a lot of intelligence, and often paranormally talented, but not wanting to take the limelight. And of course, as a researcher I am never at liberty to reveal identity or details that could allow audiences to track back to the witnesses with whom I interact.

Other Eerie Encounters in the Quad Cities and Beyond

As you can tell by now, the Quad Cities region is a place full of strange and bizarre stories. Although there were too many to give our full attention to in this book, many were just too good not to tell you about. Think of these as a kind of dessert tray—a variety of stories that, while shorter, still leave tremendous impressions on the palate as you prepare to finish your meal. We have little doubt that you will find these as compelling as we have.

Mercer County Courthouse, Aledo, Illinois

Built in 1894, the Mercer County Courthouse has been the scene of many legal dramas over the years as well as played home to many strange occurrences. Lights turn off by themselves, and the elevator doors open and close when no one has pressed the button. An X-ray machine used for security has been known to turn on and off when no one is operating it. Other unexplained activity includes doors slamming shut on their own during nightly committee meetings and mysterious footsteps heard running down the hallways.

The staff, rather affectionately, calls their apparent ghost "Sam." In 1937, during the restoration of the structure's crumbling cement supports, a buried skeleton was dug up in the basement. The remains were believed to be that of John Campbell, a pioneer who supposedly died on his way to California. He was buried along the prairie on the spot where the courthouse would be built.

Could this be the spectral Sam, accidentally disturbed from his rest?

The Painted Man, Aledo, Illinois

Only a few short blocks away from the courthouse, a city resident told us their ghost story on condition of anonymity. For years, her family had a ghost in their backyard. "We call him the Painted Man. He would just be standing around the kids, and sometimes he would try to communicate, but it wasn't English that he spoke. He was never scary to the kiddos, except one time that he was loud. I have never seen him. I've heard noises of movement but nothing else."

East Moline Public Library

The century-old East Moline Public Library has a reputation for being haunted. One story from the building alleges that a staff member saw a stuffed animal get thrown across the Children's Section when no one else was near the toy. Other stories include staff and visitors having felt the presence of an old man who haunts the mystery section.

The stories have attracted groups of local ghost researchers, including the Illinois Paranormal Research Group and Rock Island Paranormal. Both organizations found intriguing evidence of activity in the building. While investigating the Children's Section, the Illinois Paranormal Research Group captured an audio recording in which a child's voice is heard, but no children were present when it was recorded. A flashlight was also seen to turn itself on and off.

Ariel Young from the Rock Island Paranormal did her first investigation there. It made quite the impression and became one of her favorite sites. "We had quite a few spots where there were high EMFs that the K2 had picked up, but we couldn't explain them. We heard books falling off shelves, but there were no books that had fallen. We heard some disembodied voices, but we couldn't make them out."

She continued, "The camera we had set up in the head librarian's office—we heard that she passed away quite a few years before, she was an older lady. She loved the library so very much, it was like a second home. The camera caught the chair moving from one side of the desk to the other side of the desk, pushing itself and pulling itself out. That really threw me for a loop, since it was my first investigation."

St. Anthony's Nursing and Rehabilitation Center, Rock Island, Illinois

"I do know that St. Anthony's Nursing Home in Rock Island is haunted," said a former employee who didn't want to be identified. "I still remember walking into a nun's room and then went into their bathroom, and to my terror, I saw in the mirror a ghost, a woman was looking directly at me. Her hand held out at me laughing and shaking her arm at me. A lot of people have seen or heard strange things while working there. On one of the floors, while working late at night, you can even see the spirits of a person who died there being dragged through the hallway by the hair on top of their head."

Dead Man's Curve, Warren County, Illinois

Mark Manuel, program director and radio host with Q106.5 FM in the Quad Cities, has heard more than a few ghost stories in his time. Out of all of them, one in particular stands out. "A few miles east of Monmouth, Illinois, on the original Highway 34, there is a curve that has been the site of a few car accidents," he related. "At the midpoint of the curve, there is a tree that a few cars have been wrapped around. The tree is supposed to move without the help of the wind, almost as if it is trying to cause another accident."

Old Hershey Street Hospital, Muscatine, Iowa

Another story listeners told Mr. Manuel involved the Old Hershey Street Hospital in Muscatine, Iowa. "Sometimes you will be walking past the old hospital and the curtains will flutter, or you might catch a glimpse of movement through the balcony. It was present during the Civil War times, and the owner says that sometimes he hears a stumble or a person limping at night."

Buckhorn, Jackson County, Iowa

At last count, Iowa has ten ghost towns. By definition, a ghost town is an abandoned village or town, usually due to an economic collapse or a natural or human-caused disaster. The nearest such town to the Quad Cities metro area is Buckhorn, about forty-five minutes north near the city of Maquoketa.

According to the *Vintage News*, Buckhorn was a farming co-op that was bought by a dairy in 1962. There's not much left to Buckhorn but a well-maintained cemetery, a creamery building and a long-abandoned church. One of the buildings has graffiti that reads "Satan's Playground," which makes the place seem like it is straight out of a horror movie.

Please note: It is your responsibility to acquire appropriate permissions before investigating any location listed. Private property should be respected at all times, as should all posted signs concerning trespassing, hours of operation and other local regulations. Many ghost hunters have been arrested because they failed to contact property owners and/or local authorities ahead of time.

If you do decide to go, take 61 up to Maquoketa and hang a left on 64. There are plenty of cool sights and photo opportunities without having to step foot inside any of the buildings.

Crescent Bakery, Davenport, Iowa

Crescent Bakery was part of the Crescent Warehouse Historic District, which is located between East Fourth Street and Pershing Avenue. It's connected with the Rock Island Railroad bridge that spans between Davenport and the Rock Island Arsenal. The historic district is a collection of multi-story brick structures that formerly housed warehouses and factories.

The buildings in the district continued to house a variety of businesses over the years. Although its ownership changed several times, the Crescent Macaroni and Cracker Company remained in operation in 1991. The district was listed in the National Register of Historic Places in 2003.

During the transformation of the building from a bakery into loft apartments, a former owner heard a story about the bakery. One of the former maintenance workers at the bakery claimed that the building had been haunted for many years. Several years before, someone had allegedly fallen down an elevator shaft. The fall killed them, and their ghost had wandered the halls of the building ever since.

The Smith-Murphy Octagon House, Davenport, Iowa

The Octagon House was one of a few such homes built in the Quad Cities, and it is, unfortunately, the only one that still remains today. It is said to have been a stop on the Underground Railroad, a clandestine network of people, homes and businesses that helped transport runaway slaves into northern states and Canada. According to legend, one such slave died in the house, and if the conditions are just right, you can still hear them screaming.

In the 1970s, a young man was visiting the owners of the home. As they began to approach the stairs leading up the hillside to the front porch, they distinctly heard the sound of footsteps crunching through the fallen leaves in the yard. Try as he might, the young visitor couldn't see any cause for the footsteps.

Cassie Steffen of the Broadway Paranormal Society had her own experience at the home. In the summer of 2019, she took a photo of the house during the daylight hours. Later, while examining the picture, she noticed that on the second-floor window, between the trees, the faint image of two little boys can be seen. At the time of the photo, no one was living at the residence.

Village Theater, Davenport, Iowa

Village Theater, located in the beautiful village of East Davenport, started its long life as the East Davenport Turner Hall. Over the past decades, it has seen more than its fair share of historical events "The Village Theater in East Davenport is the site of the largest raid in Davenport history," said Nick Simon of Broadway Paranormal Society, which did an investigation of the place in 2019. "They were running an illegal bar out of the basement."

During the Prohibition era, it was illegal to sell, make or transport any kind of alcohol. Of course, that didn't mean that it wasn't in high demand. Illegal bars popped up all across the United States. In 1928, a federal Prohibition officer and several Davenport police officers seized 4,185 bottles of homebrew, 90 gallons of mash, 15 crocks, 50 cans of malt, beer cases and other materials for making beer.

"It is a cool old building with a lot of history to it," said Nick.

Cassie Steffen said that her group has used dowsing rods during their paranormal study of the former Turner Hall. "We ask yes or no questions with those," she said. "Cross for yes, open for no. A friend of Nick's went and hid; he went upstairs and was in a closet. Nobody knew where he was at. We started asking the spirits if they wanted to play hide-and-seek and go find the guy. We started asking, 'Is he down in the basement?' No. We went walking around. Are we getting closer to him? 'Yes.' Finally, it led us up to the steps, and we found Nick's friend. They played hide-and-seek with us through the dowsing rods."

Afterword

Hey thanks for checking out *Eerie Quad Cities* by Michael McCarty and John Brassard Jr., the follow-up to another great read, *Ghosts of the Quad Cities* (by Michael McCarty and Mark McLaughlin). My name is Rick Lopez, and along with my wife, Kathy, we own Igor's Bistro in Rock Island, which was featured in Mr. McCarty's first nod to the spooks that hang out in the Quad Cities.

Anyhow, there have been some interesting incidents since we last talked! For example, one morning, the opening cook entered the kitchen to find all our plastic Tupperware containers neatly stacked on top of one another in the middle of the floor. Now I would normally cry hoax, but I was the last one out of the building the night before.

Rick and Kathy Lopez, co-owners of Igor's Bistro, celebrating their second anniversary on April 4, 2019. This year-round Halloween-themed family-owned restaurant is located at 3055 Thirty-Eighth Street, Rock Island. The one-hundred-plus-year-old building is the home to a spirit named Toby. *Courtesy of Igor's Bistro.*

In another strange thing that happened, we had this new hire—it was her first day of working on the job. She was at the back door getting ready to start work that day when she heard a voice from the basement say, "Get out!" I was cooking at the grill, and she looked really freaked out.

I asked her, "What's the matter?"

And she said, "Someone just told me to get out."

I simply said, "Chloe, go down to the basement and introduce yourself and tell that old spook that you cannot 'get out' because it is your first day as an Igor's employee." Which she did, and since that day, there haven't been any other incidents.

There are some other weird and creepy things I could tell you as well. Stop by the restaurant sometime, and if we have some free time, we'll talk. But in the meantime, thank you for supporting Igor's Bistro and reading *Eerie Quad Cities*. God bless!

—Rick Lopez,
Co-owner of Igor's Bistro

Bibliography

BOOKS

Anderson, Fredrick, ed. *Joined by a River: Quad Cities.* Davenport, IA: Lee Enterprises, 1982.

Brassard, John, and John Brassard Jr. *Scott County Cemeteries.* Images of America series. Charleston, SC: Arcadia Publishing, 2011

Brassard, John, Jr. *Murder & Mayhem in Scott County Iowa.* Charleston, SC: The History Press, 2018.

Carlson, Bruce. *Ghosts of Scott County, Iowa.* Fort Madison, IA: Quixote Press, 1987.

Downer, Harry E. *A History of Davenport and Scott County, Iowa.* Vol. 2. Chicago: S.J. Clarke Publishing Company, 1910.

Hess, Jason. *So You Still Want to Be a Ghost Hunter?* Elmira, NY: DragonEye Publishing, 2013.

Highland Park Historical District History & Architecture. Rock Island: City of Rock Island, Illinois, 2004.

Kleen, Michael. *Haunting the Prairie: A Tourists Guide to the Weird and Wild Places of Illinois.* 1st ed. Black Oak Press, 2010.

Lewis, Chad, and Noah Voss. *Pepie: The Lake Monster of the Mississippi River.* Eau Claire, WI: Road Publications, 2014.

Lewis, Chad, and Terry Fisk. *Iowa Road Guide to Haunted Locations*. Eau Claire, WI: Unexplained Research Publishing Company, 2007.

McCarty, Michael, and Connie Corcoran Wilson. *Ghostly Tales of Route 66*. Wever, IA: Quixote Press, 2008.

McCarty, Michael, and Mark McLaughlin. *Ghosts of the Quad Cities*. Charleston, SC: The History Press, 2019.

McCarty, Michael, and The Amazing Kreskin. *Conversations with Kreskin*. West Caldwell, NJ: Team Kreskin Productions LLC, 2012.

Pohlen, Jerome. *Oddball Iowa: A Guide to Some Really Strange Places*. Chicago: Chicago Review Press, 2005.

Powers-Douglas, Minda. *Chippiannock Cemetery*. Images of America series. Charleston, SC: Arcadia Publishing, 2010.

Smith, Doug. *Davenport*. Postcard History: Iowa. Charleston, SC: Arcadia Publishing, 2007.

Swope, Robin S. *Eerie Erie*. Charleston, SC: The History Press, 2011.

Trollinger, Vernon. *Haunted Iowa City*. Charleston, SC: The History Press, 2011.

Vulich, Nick. *Gruesome Iowa: Murder, Madness and the Macabre in the Hawkeye State*. Davenport, IA: Lulu, 2019.

ARTICLES, WEBSITES AND OTHER NOTES

Preface

Rock Island Dispatch-Argus. "Famous Folks Tied to the Quad Cities." July 25, 2010.

Ronald Reagan Presidential Library and Museum. www.reaganlibrary.gov.

White, Cait. "31 Things You Probably Didn't Know About Quad Cities." *Movoto Blog*, August 26, 2014.

Willard Lamb Velie. www.wikipedia.com

Wolfe, Rich. *Joe Maddon: We're Gonna Party Like It's 1908*. N.p.: Lone Wolfe Press, 2016.

Wundram, Bill. "When Walt Didn't Make Job Cut in Davenport." *Quad-City Times*, November 17, 2003.

Abandoned and Haunted: Grandview Terrace

Gaul, Alma. "Once-Elegant Retirement Home Has Been Demolished." *Quad-City Times*, April 9, 2018.

Luna, Kay. "Grandview Terrace Empties, Piece by Piece Auction." *Quad-City Times*, July 3, 2015.

Willard, John. "Grandview Terrance Was a Royal Residence." *Quad-City Times*, June 18, 2015.

The Freemasons of the Quad Cities

Concert Archives. www.concertarchives.org.

Davenport Democrat and Leader. "Eight Years of Planning for New Bldg." November 19, 1923.

———. "New Masonic Temple Building Is Now Being Rushed to Completion." May 20, 1923.

———. "New $1,000,000 Masonic Temple Will Be Erected in Davenport." June 21, 1921.

———. "Site Purchased for Temple in 1915—$45,000." November 19, 1923.

———. "To Open Auditorium, New Temple December 10." October 21, 1923.

———. "Will Complete Local Temple by September." May 20, 1923.

Iowa Haunted Houses. "Masonic Temple—Real Davenport Haunt." www.iowahauntedhouses.com.

Turner, Jonathan. "The Big Story: Who Are the Biggest Musical Acts to Perform in the Quad-Cities?" *Quad-City Times*, March 12, 2019.

ROCK ISLAND, ILLINOIS: SKELLINGTON MANOR

The Rock Island Preservation Society article by Diane Oestreich about the Masonic Temple in Rock Island is slightly modified from the original, which appeared in the *Rock Island Argus* and *Moline Dispatch* on October 5, 2003.

The Haunted Furniture Store

Facebook. "Haunted YMCA Rock Island." http://www.facebook.com/hauntedYMCARockIsland.

Hayden, Sarah. "Paranormal Team Investigates Hauntings." *Rock Island Argus* and *Moline Dispatch*, October 27, 2018.

Moline Dispatch. "Murphy, VI. Will Arraign Jones Murder Suspect in Moline Monday." August 23, 1969.

Times-Democrat. "RI Man Is Charged in Barman's Murder." August 23, 1969.

The Mysterious Fisherman of Credit Island

Kirk, Jane. "Story of Credit Island Linked Closely with Davenport History; Was Site of Battle During 1814." *Davenport Democrat and Leader*, August 3, 1930.

The Tinsmith Ghost of Rock Island

Ancestry.com. Illinois, County Marriage Records, 1800–1940.

———. Illinois, Wills and Probate Records, 1772–1999.

Evening Democrat-Gazette. "Rock Island's Ghost." August 10, 1887.

Rock Island Argus. "Removal." March 15, 1887.

———. "Stroehle's Spirit." August 9, 1887.

Alice French House

Horton, Loren N. "French, Alice Virginia (March 19, 1830–March 9, 1934)." *The Biographical Dictionary of Iowa*. Digital edition. University of Iowa.

Koymasky, Matt, and Andrej Koymasky. "Biographies: Octave Thanet." November 18, 2008. http://andrejkoymasky.com.

Paulson, D. "There's Nothing More Terrifying than These 10 Genuinely Haunted Houses in Iowa." October 23, 2016. onlyinyourstate.com.

Switch, Callum. "Alice French House." Haunted Places. hauntedplaces.com.

Renwick Mansion

Gaul, Alma. "'I Can Envision People Living in Here and Being Happy with It': Old Pine Knoll Will Become Senior Apartments." *Dispatch-Argus*, July 16, 2019.

Hancock, Amanda. "Follow-Up File: Under New Ownership, Renwick Mansion Starts New Traditions." *Quad City Times*, April 22, 2018.

Curious Creatures

Cochran, Ky. "Mississippi River Monster Sighted Near Muscatine—or So the Legend Says According to New Book." *Muscatine Journal*, July 11, 2014.

Cook, Linda. "'Fish Guy' Swims in Celebrity After He Carried Catfish Downtown." *Quad-City Times*, April 5, 2019.

Cullen, Jack. "Big Story: Moline's Sylvan Island Mounts Surging Comeback." *Quad-City Times*, January 31, 2019.

———. "Davenport Angler Lands 55-Pound Catfish Near Credit Island." *Quad-City Times*, June 30, 2018.

Daily Times. "Rosaris Carlino Loses Life in River; Leaves Wife and Babe in Italy." December 13, 1923.

Haas, Jeremiah. "Finding Grandpa's Giant Catfish." *Quad-City Times*, May 16, 2017.

———. "A Hidden Fishery on the Mississippi River." *Rock Island Argus* and *Moline Dispatch*, September 3, 2019.

Schmidt, Kevin. "Davenport Man Reels in 60-Pound Catfish." *Quad-City Times*, June 30, 2017.

Shafer, Sheila. "Sylvan Island." Haunted Illinois website. https://www.hauntedillinois.com.

Times-Democrat. "Power Co Buys Century-Old Firm." December 7, 1966.

Death Curve: The Legend of Julia Markham

Brown, Shane. "Forget the Death Curve; Where Is That Hellcat?" *Dispatch* and *Rock Island Argus*, October 27, 2014.

———. "Is the Death Curve of Cambridge Really Haunted?" *Dispatch* and *Rock Island Argus*, October 20, 2014.

———. "Setting Out to Uncover the Truth About Death Curve of Cambridge." *Dispatch* and *Rock Island Argus*, October 19, 2014.

Find A Grave. www.findagrave.com.

Hancock, Amanda. "Big Story: Exploring 'Haunted' Places Just in Time for Halloween." *Quad-City Times*, October 22, 2018.

Kleen, M.A. "Cries from the Grave: The Cambridge Death Curve, Part 2." September 29, 2017. www.michaelkleen.com.

———. "Tragedy and Lore of Death Curve." December 4, 2018. michaelkleen.com.

———. "An Unspeakable Crime: The Cambridge Death Curve, Part 1." September 28, 2017. www.michaelkleen.com.

Marriage Records: Illinois Marriages. Various County of Illinois collections.

Monmouth Daily Atlas. "Entire Family of Nine Slain." October 4, 1905.

U.S. Census records. Year: 1900; Census Place: Oxford, Henry, Illinois; Page: 12; Enumeration District: 0026; FHL microfilm: 1240306.

Chippiannock Cemetery

Doak, Jill, ed. *Chippiannock Cemetery: 150 Years of Epitaphs.* Rock Island, IL: independently published, 2006.

Premonitions of Doom

Asheville Citizen-Times. July 6, 1898.

Daily Times. "Judge Dillon Here." October 31, 1902.

Davenport Daily Times. July 7, 1898.

Davenport Democrat and Leader. "A Handsome Monument." September 6, 1901.

———. "A Hard Blow." July 13, 1898.

———. "Historical Magazine Tells Story of Judge John F. Dillon." October 6, 1929.

———. July 7, 1898.

———. July 6, 1898.

———. July 3, 1914.

———. September 3, 1898.

———. "A Tribute." April 23, 1900.

———. "Two Handsome Features of Oakdale Cemetery." October 21, 1906.

Finch, Hortense. "That Amazing Man Named Dillon." *Quad-City Times,* October 12, 1965.

Gillette, Greg. "Central Jersey's Hero of the Bourgogne." *My Central Jersey,* July 3, 2010. https://www.mycentraljersey.com.

Morning Astorian. July 7, 1898.

New York Times. "La Bourgogne Sinks at Sea." July 7, 1898.
———. September 7, 1898.
The Observer. September 25, 1898.
Ocean Treasures. www.oceantreasures.org.
Quad-City Times. "Oakdale Monument Tells Sea Tragedy." June 19, 1955.

The Giant of Scott County

Davenport Democrat and Leader. "Cloth Masks to Combat the Flu." October 1, 1918.
———. "700 Pound Scott County Giant Who Died of Flu." December 11, 1918.
Iowa Pathways. "The Great Flu." www.iptv.com.
Langton, Diane. "Time Machine: Flu Killed More than 6,000 Iowans in 1918." *Cedar Rapids Gazette*, February 18, 2018.
Ramaciti, Dave. "The Legend of Fatty Orndorff." *Focus*, March 18, 1973.
Vergano, Dan. "1918 Flu Pandemic that Killed 50 Million Originated in China, Historians Say." *National Geographic*, January 24, 2014.
Wundrum, Bill. "He Ate the Whole Thing." *Quad-City Times*, November 28, 1985.

Other Eerie Encounters in the Quad Cities and Beyond

B100 Quad Cities. "This Terrifying Iowa Ghost Town Is Just 45 Minutes from the Quad Cities." October 3, 2017. www.b100quadcities.com.
Gorah, David. "10 Abandoned Ghost Towns in Iowa, United States—Pretty Cool and Creepy at the Same Time." Vintage News, December 3, 2015. vintagenews.com.
Robinson, Deb. "Ghost of Sam: Is the Mercer County Courthouse Haunted?" *Rock Island Argus* and *Moline Dispatch*, November 8, 2010 (updated April 25, 2014).
Rock Island Argus. "Rock Island County, 1915 Year in Review." Available on genealogytrails.com.
Shelton, Gerold. "EM Library Hosts Ghosts, Investigation Finds." *Rock Island Argus* and *Moline Dispatch*, November 8, 2017.
Smoldt, Carla. "Scary Stories from the Courthouse." *Aldeo Times Record*, December 1, 2014.

Wikipedia. "Crescent Warehouse Historic District." https://en.wikipedia.org/wiki/Crescent_Warehouse_Historic_District.

————. "Village of East Davenport." https://en.wikipedia.org/wiki/Village_of_East_Davenport.

Wundram, Bill. "A Time We Remember: Celebrating a Century in Our Quad Cities." *Quad-City Times*, 1999.

About the Authors

JOHN BRASSARD JR. is a local author, podcaster and historian. He has written two books on local history: *Scott County Cemeteries* (co-written with his father, John Brassard Sr.) and *Murder and Mayhem in Scott County, Iowa*. His work has appeared in several places, including the *Iowa History Journal*, the *Quad-City Times*, the *North Scott Press* and the *DeWitt Observer*. Mr. Brassard is also the writer, researcher and narrator for the *Kitchen Table Historian* podcast, which tells tales of true crime, the paranormal and other stories that your grandma didn't want you to hear. His website is http://johnbrassardjr.com. Find him on Facebook at http://www.facebook. com/kitchentablehistorian.

John Brassard Jr. at the Mount Joy Cemetery in Long Grove, Iowa. *Photo by Michael McCarty.*

MICHAEL MCCARTY has been a professional writer since 1983 and is the author of more than forty books of fiction and nonfiction, including *Frankenstein's Mistress: Tales of Love & Monsters*, *Dark Cities: Dark Tales*, *I Kissed a Ghoul*, *A Little Help from My Fiends*, *Dark Duets*, *Liquid Diet & Midnight Snack*, *Dracula Transformed and Other Bloodthirsty Tales* (also with Mark McLaughlin) and *Lost Girl of the Lake* (with Joe McKinney). He is a five-time Bram Stoker Award finalist and in 2008 won the David R. Collins Literary Achievement Award from the Midwest Writing Center. He also author of the giant book of interviews *Modern Mythmakers: 35 Interviews with Horror and Science Fiction Writers and Filmmakers*, which features interviews with Ray Bradbury, Dean Koontz, John Carpenter, Richard Matheson, Elvira, Linnea Quigley, John Saul, Joe McKinney and many more. He also wrote *Ghostly Tales of Route 66* (co-written with Connie Corcoran Wilson) and *Ghost of the Quad Cities* (with Mark McLaughlin). Michael McCarty lives

Michael McCarty at the Mount Joy Cemetery in Long Grove, Iowa. *Photo by John Brassard Jr.*

in Rock Island, Illinois, with his wife, Cindy, and pet rabbit, Yeti. Michael McCarty is on Twitter at michaelmccarty6. His blog site is at http://monstermikeyaauthor.wordpress.com. Find him on Facebook at http://www.facebook.com/michaelmccartyhorror and the "Ghosts of the Quad Cities" Facebook page: http://www.facebook.com/qcghosts.

Visit us at
www.historypress.com